Cheap and Easy Cooking
with Wines,
Liquors, and Liqueurs

Cheap and Easy Cooking
with Wines,
Liquors, and Liqueurs

by Jennifer Stone

DOUBLEDAY & COMPANY, INC., GARDEN CITY, NEW YORK

1974

ISBN: 0-385-06596-5
Library of Congress Catalog Card Number 73–83677
Copyright © 1972 by Jennifer Stone
Printed in the United States of America
First Edition in the United States of America

FOR PETER WITH LOVE

Acknowledgments

Anybody who cooks does so for two reasons: to survive or to ensure the survival of others, and to delight.

Those of us who cook to delight learn our skills everywhere, and I am grateful to my teachers—starting with my mother, who encouraged me to cook almost as soon as she encouraged me to read, and continuing on to all the people who have written cookbooks and articles that have amused, inspired, outraged, and titillated me.

In the first year of being married, my bedtime reading was always a cookbook, much to the amusement of my husband, who couldn't understand the pleasure to be had from reading about food as opposed to eating it.

And I am grateful to my husband, who ate everything I made, helped me and bullied me away from the ambitious three-course dinners that were never ready until midnight. I'm only sorry his waistline suffered.

I'm also very grateful to all my friends who swapped boozy recipes, and who helped me reject all complicated and pretentious recipes. Everything in this book is as uncomplicated as possible.

Without Jane Hoyle's help this book would have been finished, but heaven knows when.

Thank you all.

Contents

Introduction

Why eat it when you can drink it? Why should anyone pour good alcohol into a cooking pot?

Because it's the simplest way of turning yourself into the sort of cook who is the envy of all the people lucky enough to be invited by her or him to dinner.

Because it's the quickest way of producing a superlative meal.

And because, believe it or not, it is frequently the *cheapest* way of producing something out of the ordinary.

And there are beneficial side effects as well. If you're cooking with a bottle of sherry, wine, beer, or whatever at your elbow, you might as well take a drink at the same time as you add a little to your recipe. Hence it is being used to improve your masterpiece, and your temper. Happiness all around. And the happy cook is the good cook.

So if you're like me, this method is for you. Much as I love cooking, dearly as I love my friends, I do also have a baby to care for, a house to run, to say nothing of a job. So if ever I am to see a film, read a book, climb a mountain, or write a letter, my cooking has to be speedy. It has to fit in with other things.

Alcohol is the key to all this. Even in the simplest dishes. Even with something as American as that classic stand-by, roast beef.

What do I do with roast beef, for goodness' sake? Well, I do something to the gravy.

It should never taste like that thick lumpy stuff made from flour and meat cubes. Throw away all the little packets food manufacturers try to convince you are essential for producing good gravy.

In the roasting pan stir a good tablespoonful of flour into a sizable quantity of fat from the meat. Stir really well and scrape up all the bits. When everything is absorbed, add some wine and, stirring diligently, bring the gravy to a boil. If it is thick, add more wine, or vegetable water, or stock if you have any. Just before serving stir in a good dollop of cream. Quantities depend on how many you're feeding and how thin you like your gravy.

Don't worry too much about the cost. While it is obviously hopelessly extravagant to make a trip to the liquor store to buy a bottle of scotch to pour on your canned peaches, it is hardly wanton profligacy to help yourself to the equivalent of a small nip from a bottle of whatever you happen to have in the drinks cupboard. It's quite likely someone in your house does anyway. Just as you don't use a whole sack of flour at a time, neither do you pour a whole bottle of fine burgundy into a casserole with a chicken for *coq au vin.*

Never use really expensive wines for cooking. Never. Ever. Or not unless money really is as nothing to you.

Despite what many experts will tell you—in their friendly arrogance—it is not necessary to cook with the wines you plan to drink. Nor is it essential to use top-class sherry for salmon mousse, or *fine* champagne cognac for brandy butter. Sheer madness in my opinion.

So low has the quality of the wine I use for cooking sunk that I once made a beef and wine stew with nine tenths of a bottle of red plonk, opened two days before, which had turned vinegary. The result was quite delicious, and we certainly didn't feel we should have drunk vinegar with it.

The whole question of cost gets so distorted it is almost impossible to argue rationally. Some people who spend what I consider a small fortune on fillet steak and lobster reckon that I waste money when I pour white wine on cod. And while many a man will not allow his wife to use a glass of brandy for cooking, he will happily take her out to a thirty-dollar dinner and have brandy with coffee as well.

But if you are not completely broke, do want to produce above average food, but do not have half a day to prepare your better meals: try cooking my way—with alcohol.

A word of caution. I am English and have done all my cooking in Europe. In translating this book into American (a different language!) I have done my best, with the help of my patient American editor, to ensure that everything I refer to is available in your shops. Nonetheless if I should talk of 16-ounce cans of black cherries and your major brands come in 14-ounce cans, forgive me. But don't worry—the whole essence of alcoholic cooking is a casual, easy-going approach. A couple of ounces either way in many of the ingredients won't spoil the finished effect.

Starters

AVOCADOS WITH GRAPES

This is a different way of tarting up one of the old faithfuls.

3 ripe avocados
lemon juice
1½ pounds muscat grapes

7 tablespoons sweet Madeira or
sherry

Prepare the avocados as usual. Brush the insides freely with lemon juice to prevent discoloring. Chill. Halve the grapes and remove the pips. Fill the pear halves with the grapes and sprinkle with the wine.
Serves 6.

AVOCADO MOUSSE

I first had this at a restaurant and then searched just about every cookbook ever written to find out how to make it. A journalist friend finally told me—it's so easy, anyone can manage it.

3 very ripe avocados
⅔ cup sour cream
3½ tablespoons sweet sherry

salt and freshly ground black
pepper

Skin and stone the avocados. Using a silver fork, mash them until smooth. Some people liquidize them but this I don't care for: firstly the consistency is too smooth and secondly you waste an awful lot of avocado, which is sinful at the price they are. Then stir in the cream, sherry, and seasoning. Store in the fridge until needed or serve at once. If this is to be stored it must be kept in a bowl in a polythene bag or in Tupperware. If the air is not kept out, the lovely pale green color goes and you are left with an unattractive donkey brown. It's delicious, though, as avocados have a slightly liverish reputation, I wouldn't serve this before, say, chocolate gâteau.
Serves 6 (or more if the avocados are large).

JERUSALEM ARTICHOKE MOUSSE

This vegetable has never been very popular, but I think it has an interesting taste.

2 pounds Jerusalem artichokes	4 eggs
1 envelope unflavored gelatin	salt and pepper
⅔ cup water	1 cup heavy cream
3 tablespoons sherry	

Peel the artichokes and boil in salted water for about 15 minutes. Drain, mash, and sieve.

Mix the gelatin and water together and put on a low heat until the gelatin has dissolved. Add to the purée, together with the sherry, and leave to cool a little.

Separate the eggs. Lightly whisk the yolks and add to the purée. Season well and leave in a cool place until just beginning to set.

Beat the egg whites until very stiff, and also whip the cream. As the purée begins to set, fold them both in. Pour into individual ramekins or a soufflé dish. Chill.

Serves 6 to 8.

ITALIAN EGGPLANT

Can be served as a first course or as a supper dish, either hot or cold.

3 fairly large eggplants	¼ pound button mushrooms, peeled and sliced
salt	
cooking oil	¼ pound ham, chopped
1 tablespoon butter	2 tablespoons white wine or sherry
1 tablespoon flour	
⅔ cup milk	1½ tablespoons cream
½ cup grated cheese	seasoning

Preheat oven to 425° F. Cut the eggplants in half lengthwise. With a knife cut around the edge of the inside about 1 inch deep and make several insertions across the flesh in the middle. Sprinkle them with salt and leave to stand for about 1 hour. Pour off the liquid and wipe off the salt. Heat some cooking oil and sauté, turning once or twice, for about 10 minutes. Drain on absorbent paper.

Melt the butter, add flour, and stir in enough milk to make a thick white sauce. Add the cheese, reserving some to sprinkle on top of the eggplants before baking them, and stir until dissolved. Add the mushrooms, ham, white wine or sherry, and the cream, and season well.

Scoop out the middle of the eggplants, being careful not to damage the skin. Dice it and add to the sauce. Fill the eggplant skins with the mixture and sprinkle the grated cheese on top. Bake for about 7 to 10 minutes.

Serves 6.

GLOUCESTERSHIRE RAREBIT

This is a pleasant first course. If you double the quantities it makes an excellent supper dish—cheap and filling too.

½ **pound strong hard cheese**	**4 thick slices bread**
prepared mustard	**butter**
1¼ cups ale	

Preheat oven to 325° F. Flake or coarsely grate the cheese into a fireproof dish. Spread mustard to taste over the cheese and pour in the ale. Bake until the cheese is dissolved. Toast the bread, butter it, and sprinkle the buttered side with a little extra ale. Pour the sauce over and serve at once.

Serves 4.

BAKED EGGS WITH PÂTÉ

Effortless, delicious, and just the thing to use up spare pâté.

butter
4 ¼-inch slices fine pâté, i.e.
   chicken liver, foie gras, kipper,
   or sardine
salt and plenty of pepper

4 tablespoons liquor to match
   pâté, i.e. brandy with chicken
   liver, Madeira with foie gras,
   white wine with kipper
4 or 8 eggs

Preheat oven to 350° F. Butter four ramekins extremely generously (otherwise the washing up will be hell). Place a round of pâté in the bottom of each. Be liberal with the salt and pepper. Pour on the liquor. Gently break in 1 or 2 eggs to taste (i.e. depending on how substantial the rest of the meal is to be). Stand in a roasting tin of hot water and bake for 15 minutes.
Serves 4.

BAKED EGGS WITH MUSTARD, CHEESE, AND WINE

This is exceptionally good.

½ cup grated Gruyère cheese
2½ teaspoons Dijon mustard
2½ tablespoons dry white wine
salt

1 cup sour cream
12 eggs
buttered bread crumbs

Preheat oven to 350° F. Mix the cheese, mustard, wine, and salt with the cream.

Grease six individual ramekins with buttered paper. Break 2 eggs into each and top with the sauce and sprinkle with bread crumbs. Stand the ramekins in a roasting tin half filled with water and bake for 15 minutes.
Serves 6.

EGGS BAKED IN MUSHROOM SAUCE

More unusual than eggs baked in cream and a pleasant change.

½ pound button mushrooms
6 tablespoons butter
2 tablespoons flour
1¼ cups dry white wine ⎱ or 2½ cups dry white wine
1¼ cups chicken stock ⎰

3½ tablespoons good mayonnaise
2 chives, chopped
several sprigs parsley, chopped
salt and pepper
6 eggs
4 tablespoons butter
½ cup grated Gruyère cheese

Preheat oven to 375° F. Wash the mushrooms if necessary and then slice them finely. Melt the 6 tablespoons butter and sauté the mushrooms until they are brown all over. Then work in the flour. When this has all been absorbed, gradually add the wine and stock, and mix in the mayonnaise, chives, and parsley. Add salt and pepper to taste and cook for a further 5 minutes.

Pour into six individual ramekins. Break an egg into the center of each, melt the remaining 4 tablespoons butter, and pour a little over each egg. Sprinkle with the cheese. Stand the ramekins in a pan of warm water and bake until cooked—about 5 minutes.

Serves 6.

EGG, AVOCADO, AND SHERRY MOUSSE

I find this one of the most delicious ways of starting a meal.

2 avocados—they must be ripe
juice of 1 small lemon
6 hard-cooked eggs
salt and pepper
⅔ cup good mayonnaise
1½ envelopes unflavored gelatin

enough water to dissolve it
1 cup heavy cream
2 tablespoons sweet sherry
½ tin anchovy fillets for
   decoration

Cut the avocados in half, remove the stones, scoop out the flesh, and mash it with a silver fork. Stir in the lemon juice to prevent the flesh changing color. Use as little as possible.

Shell the eggs and chop them finely. Add salt and pepper to taste and stir in the mayonnaise. Dissolve the gelatin in the water.

Whip the cream in a large bowl until it starts to thicken, then stir in the sherry and gelatin. Add the avocados and the eggs and mix the lot thoroughly. Turn into a straight-sided bowl and leave in the fridge to set. Unmold just before serving, decorate with anchovies, and surround with, say, a simple tomato salad lightly dressed.

Serves 6.

EXTRA SPECIAL SCRAMBLED EGGS

Perhaps shouldn't be served for breakfast, but an unusual variation on a theme.

4 eggs
grated rind of ½ orange
dash of sherry
salt and pepper

1½ tablespoons heavy cream
2 tablespoons butter
hot buttered toast

Beat eggs lightly with a fork and add most of the grated rind, the sherry, seasoning, and cream. Melt the butter, add the eggs, and cook slowly, stirring constantly with a wire whisk, until they achieve a rich creamy consistency. Serve the eggs on hot buttered toast with a little grated orange on top.

Serves 2 to 3.

GRILLED GRAPEFRUIT

This is a variation on Britain's dullest first course: half a grapefruit with a maraschino cherry in the middle.

2 grapefruit
a little sherry or Madeira
brown sugar

Halve the grapefruit and prepare in the usual way, loosening all the segments. Sprinkle with a little sherry and a thin layer of sugar. Put under a hot grill until the sugar is dissolved and serve immediately.

This can also be served as a dessert.

Serves 4.

GRAPEFRUIT WITH GIN

You might well think this is an odd combination, but try it and sample its interesting flavor.

3 grapefruit
6 tablespoons gin

Prepare the grapefruit as usual and pour a spoonful of gin over each half. It is unnecessary to add any sugar unless one has a very sweet tooth.

Serves 6.

MELON CRESCENTS

These make a delicious beginning to a heavy meal.

1 honeydew melon	**water**
1 11-ounce can mandarin oranges	**1 package strawberry- or**
3 tablespoons or 1 miniature	**raspberry-flavored gelatin**
bottle Grand Marnier	

Cut the melon in half and remove seeds. Cut out as many perfect melon balls as possible. With a spoon remove the rest of the flesh (keep this for a fruit salad or the children's supper). Drain the mandarin oranges, reserving the juice. Stand each melon shell on a large piece of foil. Fill them with a mixture of melon balls and mandarins. Mix the Grand Marnier with enough water to make up 1¼ cups. Pour over the gelatin in a pan and warm gently until dissolved. Divide the liquid between the two shells, wrap them up, and store in the fridge until well set. Cut each piece into three.
Serves 6.

MUSHROOM AND CHICKEN-LIVER OMELET

This filling can be prepared beforehand and kept warm, so all you have to do at the last minute is make the omelet.

⅛ pound sliced mushrooms	**2 tablespoons**
¼ cup butter	**consommé**
1 small shallot	**2 tablespoons**
4 chicken livers	**dry white**
salt and pepper	**wine**
½ teaspoon flour	**2 6-egg omelets**

or 4 tablespoons either one

Sauté the mushrooms in 1 tablespoon butter for about 4 to 5 minutes. Remove and keep warm. Chop the shallot finely, slice the chicken livers, and sauté both in the remaining butter for less than a minute, being careful not to let the livers get hard or the shallot burn. Season well, add the flour, and stir for a minute. Then add the consommé and wine. Stir well and add the mushrooms. Keep warm until the omelets are ready.

Make the omelets; when nearly cooked spread the mixture over one half of the omelets and fold in the usual way.

Serves 8 as a starter or 4 for supper.

MUSHROOMS IN CREAM

This can also be served as an accompanying vegetable.

1 pound white button mushrooms	1 cup heavy cream
1¼ cups water	2 tablespoons dry white wine
salt	ground pepper

Wash the mushrooms and remove the stalks. Boil the water with the salt. Add the mushrooms and cook gently for 3 to 4 minutes. Meanwhile heat the cream in a separate pan together with the wine; do not boil. Drain the mushrooms and add them to the cream. Cook for 2 or 3 minutes and serve immediately with freshly milled black pepper.

Serves 4.

CHILLED MUSHROOM COCKTAIL

*Not something you'll have had boringly often. No culinary skills
needed to make it.*

¾ pound white button
   mushrooms
¼ small onion
½ cup heavy cream
3 tablespoons good mayonnaise

2 tablespoons dry white wine
1 tablespoon anchovy essence
seasoning
lemon slices

Wash the mushrooms and slice finely. Peel and chop the onion
very small. Whip the cream until thickened.

Make the sauce by mixing together the mayonnaise, cream,
onion, wine, and anchovy essence. Season well and chill for about
30 minutes. Add the mushrooms and spoon into individual glasses.
Chill. Decorate with slices of lemon. Serve with brown bread and
butter.

Serves 4 to 5.

MUSHROOMS À LA GRECQUE

One of the best cold courses in anybody's repertoire.

4½ tablespoons oil, preferably
   olive
1 large onion, chopped
1 clove garlic, crushed
⅔ cup dry white wine
bouquet garni

salt and freshly milled pepper
1 pound firm mushrooms
4 peeled and seeded tomatoes
2½ tablespoons olive oil
masses of chopped parsley—at
   least 2 handfuls

Heat the 4½ tablespoons of oil and sauté the onion and garlic until
they are soft. Stir in the wine, bouquet garni, salt, and pepper.
Peel the mushrooms and add them to the pan, together with the
tomatoes. Cook gently for about 15 minutes. Chill. Just before

serving, remove the bouquet garni and stir in the 2½ tablespoons of oil and the parsley.

Serves 4 to 6.

You can make this without the tomatoes, or with a little lemon juice or with cloves. All just as good.

ORANGE VINAIGRETTE

A refreshing start to a meal. Make in advance but do not pour vinaigrette over the oranges until the last minute.

6 large oranges	1½ tablespoons orange liqueur
6½ tablespoons olive oil	seasoning
2 tablespoons wine vinegar	1½ tablespoons chopped parsley
1½ teaspoons finely chopped onion	

Peel the oranges, removing all the pith, and slice horizontally. Arrange on a serving dish. Make the dressing by mixing together the oil, vinegar, onion, orange liqueur, and seasoning. Pour over the oranges and sprinkle with parsley.

Serves 6.

APPETIZING PEARS

Another fruity first course to provide a light start to a meal.

4 ripe pears	salt and pepper
lemon juice	1¼ tablespoons chopped parsley
5 tablespoons heavy cream	¼ pound ham, chopped
1 tablespoon sweet sherry	lettuce leaves
¼ pound cream cheese	

Peel, slice, and core the pears. Dip them in lemon juice so that they don't discolor. Whip the cream with the sherry and mix with the cream cheese. Season. Fold in the parsley and finely chopped ham. Pile the mixture on top of the pears and arrange on the lettuce leaves.

Serves 4 (or 8 if the pears are enormous).

CREAMED SPINACH WITH MADEIRA

This can be served as a separate course or as a vegetable.

2 pounds spinach	2½ tablespoons heavy cream
water	¼ pound mushrooms
butter	2 tablespoons Madeira
nutmeg	diced white bread
salt and pepper	

Cook the spinach in the water for about 10 minutes, or until just soft. Drain thoroughly, squeezing all the water out. Chop into small pieces and once again drain off any excess water. Add 1 tablespoon butter, a little nutmeg, salt and pepper, and the cream. Sauté the mushrooms in some butter for a few minutes and add them to the spinach, together with the Madeira. Sauté some diced white bread in some butter until the croutons are golden brown and crisp. Reheat the spinach and sprinkle it with the croutons before serving.
Serves 4.

KIPPER PÂTÉ

Good, easy, keeps well.

1 7-ounce can kippered herring fillets	¾ cup butter
3 tablespoons brandy	½ lemon

Drain and skin the fillets and leave to soak for an hour or so in the brandy. Melt the butter, squeeze the lemon, and put all ingredients in the blender. Switch on. When mixture is smooth turn out into serving dishes. Chill. Serve decorated with thin slices of lemon.
Serves 4 to 6.

PORK AND LIVER PÂTÉ

Rich, good and particularly rewarding for smart picnics.

½ pound calf's liver	2 tablespoons salt
½ pound chicken livers	1½ tablespoons brandy
1 pound lean pork	1 tablespoon Madeira
1 shallot, chopped	2 tablespoons chopped parsley
2 tablespoons cinnamon	strips of bacon

Preheat oven to 350° F. Mince the liver and the pork until very fine. Add the rest of the ingredients except bacon and mix well together. Line a terrine or loaf tin with strips of bacon and cover with the pâté mixture. Bake for 1½ to 2 hours. Cool the pâté with a heavy weight on top of it. Chill.
Serves 8.

It is less effort, and cheaper, to use 1½ pounds minced belly pork instead of the lean pork and the strips of bacon. Purists don't, as they like the bacon around the pâté when it is turned out, but it always seems a waste to me as so many people leave the bacon on their plates.

QUICK AND EASY CHICKEN LIVER PÂTÉ

This is incredibly easy: it takes far longer to wash up than make. Brandy or sherry are the best liquors to use, but in desperation I've used beer reasonably successfully.

6 tablespoons butter	3½ tablespoons brandy or sherry
1 large clove garlic, crushed	1 tablespoon vinegar (optional)
½ small onion, chopped	1 tablespoon Dijon mustard
½ pound chicken livers	salt and pepper

Melt the butter and sauté the garlic and onion until transparent. Add the cleaned chicken livers and cook gently for 4 or 5 minutes. Put this in a liquidizer together with the liquor, vinegar, mustard, and seasoning. Turn into a small terrine and leave to cool. Serve with hot toast and butter.
Serves 4 to 6, depending on one's appetite.

PHEASANT PÂTÉ

This is very rich, feeds about 20 people. It is not the quickest recipe in the world, but it is not in any way complicated and the finished result is heaven.

1 cooked pheasant—you can either roast it or casserole it in a little red wine	½ cup brandy
	½ cup sherry
	4 to 5 spring onions, chopped (if available)
1½ cups butter	
1 pound chicken livers	1 tablespoon homemade mustard

Take the meat off the pheasant which is by far the most fiddly part. Melt half the butter and gently sauté the chicken livers until they are pink (about 5 minutes). When the livers are cool, put them in a liquidizer, add the rest of the butter, and liquidize until smooth. If your machine will stand it, put the pheasant through the liquidizer as well, mixed with the liver to act as a lubricant. If your machine is not strong enough, mince the pheasant or chop it finely— the finished result will taste the same but have a different texture. Beat everything vigorously in a large bowl, then put the pâté mixture into the dishes from which it will be served. Keep it in the fridge, but do allow it to warm to room temperature for 3 to 4 hours before it is eaten. It will keep for some days in an ordinary fridge.

Serves 20.

PÂTÉ MOLD

*An eye-catching way of serving pâté which gives it a Fortnum &
Mason look.*

1 can consommé	½ pound good fine pâté
¼ cup sherry	(preferably homemade)
2 3-ounce packages Philadelphia	2 or 3 chives
cream cheese	unflavored gelatin if required

Heat the consommé, then add the sherry. Leave to cool. When
cool pour a depth of only ½ inch into the bottom of the mold and
leave in the fridge until set hard. Mash the cream cheese and pâté
with a fork until the mixture is smooth. Chop the chives and sprinkle onto the center of the set consommé. Put the pâté mixture on
top of this, leaving an inch free around the edge. Then pour the
rest of the consommé around and over the pâté. Leave to set in
the fridge. Turn out and serve with toast.

Serves 4 to 6.

If you want to turn this out sometime before eating, dissolve a
little gelatin in the consommé at the start.

PÂTÉ DE CAMPAGNE

This is an adaptation of my own of a traditional recipe as I like my pâtés more livery than a meat loaf.

⅓ pound liver or even more if you care to
1 pound mixed ground veal and pork
¼ pound ground ham, bacon, or beef, or omit altogether
1 to 2 cloves garlic, crushed (optional)
¼ pound chopped-up back pork fat
black pepper
salt—at least 1 teaspoon
bay leaves, parsley, orégano, mace, or whatever your favorite spice happens to be
5 tablespoons wine or, preferably, brandy
piece of fatty bacon or whatever you can cajole from your butcher to cover the pâté while it is cooking

Preheat oven to 350° F. Grind, chop, or liquidize the liver. Put all the ingredients into a big bowl and mix them very well. This is the only thing you have to do to make your pâté good. It is worth doing properly, or else give up and buy a commercially made pâté, which, unless it is very expensive, won't be much good so should inspire you to keep mixing.

If the mixture seems a little dry (which it might—the meat can vary greatly) add some more wine. It shouldn't be sloppy but it won't matter greatly if it is. Pack it in a suitable vessel (at least 1½-pint capacity), cover it well, and bake in a moderate oven for about 1½ hours. It may take longer. To see if it is cooked, poke it with a small knife and then press down alongside the slit. If blood runs out keep cooking. Let it cool and preferably keep for a day before eating. Either serve direct from the bowl or turn out and scrape off the fat.

Some people say you should let the mixture stand for an hour or two before cooking—it never seems to make the slightest odds to me, so I've given up doing so. If bay leaves are your favorite flavoring, decorate the top of the pâté with them.

This feeds 6 to 8 quite substantially.

EASY PORK AND LIVER TERRINE

Every household should have at least one of these in their freezer or freezer part of the fridge. It's simple, so good, not even fattening.

1 pound pig's liver	2½ tablespoons of any wine or
¼ pound belly of pork	any spirit except gin; or, in a
salt and pepper	pinch, cider
1 or more cloves garlic, crushed	1 strip bacon

Preheat oven to 350° F. Grind liver and pork together. Add the seasoning, garlic, and wine. Mix well. Pack it into a pint terrine or any small suitable ovenproof bowl. Cut the bacon into small squares and press them onto the mixture. Cover and bake for 1 hour in a medium oven. Then remove cover and bake for a further 10 minutes. Purists stand the terrine in a bowl of water while cooking, but it isn't necessary.

Serves 4 to 6.

TUNA PÂTÉ

If the mercury scare hasn't put you off tuna forever, you could try this easy pâté.

¾ cup butter	1 small onion
1 7-ounce can tuna	3½ tablespoons brandy
3½ tablespoons olive oil	salt and pepper
juice of a lemon	

Melt the butter. Put all the ingredients into a blender and liquidize until smooth. Turn out into serving dishes. Chill.

Ideally, take out of the fridge 1 hour before serving. Garnish with chopped hard-cooked eggs, olives, etc.

Serves 6.

SARDINE PÂTÉ

This is similar to the previous recipe. If you double the quantities and mash the sardines instead of liquidizing them you make a very nice sardine mold that can be served as a main course in the summer with a tomato salad.

¾ cup butter	1 small onion
2 tins sardines	3½ tablespoons dry sherry
3½ tablespoons olive oil	pepper
juice of a lemon	1½ tablespoons chopped parsley

Melt the butter. Put all the ingredients except parsley into a blender and switch on. When smooth stir in the parsley and turn out into a serving dish. Chill. Garnish with anchovies, chives, or what you will.
Serves 6.

SMOKED SALMON PÂTÉ

Personally I never enjoy smoked salmon pâté as much as smoked salmon, but for people with really jaded palates this is good. It is also a useful way of using up the scrappy bits if you've been lucky enough to have had a whole smoked salmon.

6 tablespoons soft butter	4½ tablespoons heavy cream
2½ tablespoons dry sherry	pinch of paprika
½ pound smoked salmon	

Put the first three ingredients into a liquidizer and blend until smooth. Then add the cream and paprika. Pour into a serving bowl and keep in the fridge until needed.
Serves 4 to 6, depending on what follows.

SHRIMP PÂTÉ

Another easy first course.

½ pound shrimps, cooked and
    shelled
2½ tablespoons lemon juice
salt and freshly ground black
    pepper

generous pinch of paprika
3½ tablespoons sherry
3½ tablespoons olive oil

Prepare the shrimps and put in a liquidizer together with the rest of the ingredients. When smooth, turn out and chill in the fridge. Serve with toast and butter.
Serves 6.

TURKEY PÂTÉ

A delicious way of using up turkey leftovers.

4 walnuts (8 halves or more if
    desired)
2½ tablespoons sherry
½ pound turkey
¼ pound ham

½ cup bread crumbs
1¼ cups chicken stock
1 envelope unflavored gelatin
salt and pepper

Marinate the walnuts in the sherry for about ½ hour. Grind the turkey and ham and mix well with the bread crumbs. Chop the nuts and add to the mixture. Heat the stock and dissolve the gelatin in it, stirring until it is quite smooth. Let this cool and then add the turkey mixture and blend well. Season to taste. Pour into a 1½-pint basin and put a heavy weight on top. Leave in a cool place. Dip the bowl in warm water, turn out, and decorate with cucumber slices or bunches of water cress.
Serves 6.

APPLE CURRY SOUP

An original recipe that is very popular—I tried it at a time when apples were coming out of my ears in the autumn and I was determined not to serve them in a dessert yet again.

2 tablespoons butter	2 egg yolks
1 medium-size onion	2 eating apples
2½ cups chicken stock	salt and pepper
1¼ tablespoons curry powder	lemon juice
1 tablespoon cornstarch	2½ tablespoons Calvados
¾ cup heavy cream	greenery to garnish

Melt the butter. Chop the onion and sauté until golden. Add the stock and curry powder, and the cornstarch mixed with a drop of water. Bring to boiling point and simmer for about 10 minutes. Heat the cream and add the egg yolks. When smooth stir slowly into the soup.

Pour the soup into a liquidizer and add a peeled and cored apple. Blend until smooth. Add a little salt and pepper to taste and then chill. Just before serving, cut up the remaining apple, sprinkle with lemon juice to stop it turning brown, and add it to the soup with the Calvados. Garnish with a little greenery.

Serves 4.

ICED AVOCADO SOUP

This is very rich but absolutely delicious.

2 ripe avocados	pinch of cayenne
½ cup sour cream or heavy cream	2½ tablespoons dry sherry
seasoning	milk
	parsley

Cut the avocados in half, remove the stones, and scoop out all the flesh. Mash, mouli or liquidize it. Then mix it with the cream, salt and pepper, and cayenne. Add the sherry and thin the mixture down with milk to the required consistency. Cover the mixture and chill. Decorate with parsley before serving.
Serves 6.

BLOODY MARY SOUP

Marvelous.

2 tablespoons butter	1 tablespoon salt
1 onion, finely chopped	2 teaspoons Worcestershire sauce
3 stalks celery, diced	¼ teaspoon pepper
2 tablespoons tomato purée	dash of lemon juice
1 tablespoon sugar	4 tablespoons vodka
5 cups tomato juice	

Melt the butter and gently sauté the onion and celery until golden brown. Stir in the tomato purée and sugar, add the tomato juice, and simmer for 10 minutes. Add the remaining ingredients. Liquidize. This can be served hot or cold.
Serves 6.

CAVIAR AND CONSOMMÉ SOUP

Light and cool and very good.

2 cans consommé	sour cream or heavy cream
3½ tablespoons dry sherry	
1 3-ounce jar lumpfish roe (mock caviar)	

Melt the consommé and add the sherry and caviar. Pour into individual dishes and leave in the fridge to jell. Serve cold with a dollop of cream on the top.
Serves 4 to 6.

ICED CHERRY SOUP

Unusual, light, and much liked.

¾ cup dry red wine	sugar if required
2 cloves	juice of 1 lemon or to taste
pared rind of ½ orange	2½ cups water
pinch of cinnamon	1½ tablespoons cornstarch
1 can black cherries in syrup	sour cream to garnish

Gently simmer the wine, cloves, orange, and cinnamon for a few minutes. Strain the wine into a fresh saucepan and add the cherries, syrup, sugar, lemon juice, and almost all the water. Bring to the boil.

Meanwhile blend the cornstarch with the remaining water and add to the soup. Simmer for about 2 minutes, stirring all the time. Pour into a container and chill. Stir well before serving. Garnish with a dollop of sour cream in each soup dish.

Serves 4.

CHESTNUT CREAM SOUP

Don't be put off by the thought of skinning the chestnuts; this soup is well worth it and is extremely economical.

¾ pound chestnuts (canned will do, but they do not taste as good)	1¼ cups milk
	6 tablespoons sherry
	parsley
3¾ cups stock	salt and pepper
2 tablespoons butter	a little cream
½ cup flour	

Slit the chestnuts and boil in water for about 10 minutes so that the skins come off easily. Peel them—this is the worst part of all, but don't give up. It is well worth it in the end. Put the shelled nuts in a saucepan together with the stock and cover and simmer for 1 hour. Liquidize. Melt the butter and add the flour, then stir in the stock and cook until it boils. Meanwhile, boil the milk and stir it into the soup. (If the chestnuts have been cooked too quickly, the soup may be too thick and it can be thinned with more milk.) Add the sherry and parsley and season with salt and pepper. A dollop of cream on the top when serving looks and tastes good.

Serves 6.

GOOD VEGETABLE SOUP

In winter it pays fantastic dividends to keep a good vegetable soup in the house. This is how to do it.

3 onions	more vegetables as desired
3 leeks	½ cup butter or oil
3 stalks celery	½ cup sherry or wine
2 potatoes	1 28-ounce can tomatoes

Peel and chop the vegetables you plan to include.

Heat the butter and gently sauté the vegetables until they soften a little. Then pour on the sherry or wine (or beer or cider) and let it get absorbed by the vegetables. Pour in the tomatoes. Stir well and add 2 to 3 cups of cold water. Bring to the boil and simmer gently until the vegetables are soft (an hour or so).

If your soup is full of large lumps of vegetables, liquidize it. If you prepared the vegetables exhaustively and it looks more like minestrone, don't.

Most people like a little grated cheese sprinkled on top of this kind of soup.

Serves at least 6.

This is a deliberately vague recipe because you can make it what you will: more carrots and it's basically carrot soup. You can add cauliflower or the better cauliflower leaves; drop in the outer leaves of a lettuce, the leftover mashed potatoes from your kid's supper, or virtually any vegetable in the house you want eaten up, or that's cheap and in season at the time. I never thicken this kind of soup as it is quite thick enough for me as it is, and anyway it's more slimming not to, but if you care to you can dissolve flour or cornstarch in a little of the liquid and stir it in; but you may well end up having to thin it down with a little water!

COLD COMFORT

And who could refuse anything with such an evocative name?

1 can consommé   1 chopped hard-cooked egg
½ cup dry sherry   chopped chives
2 tablespoons heavy cream

Chill the consommé in the fridge for some hours. Fifteen minutes
before eating, spoon half into each of two bowls. Pour the sherry
over, and the cream, and sprinkle with egg and chives.
    Serves 2.

CURRIED CREAM-CHEESE CONSOMMÉ

*A very popular recipe that couldn't be easier—serve it in ramekin
dishes and it goes farther.*

3 3-ounce packages Philadelphia   curry powder to taste
    cream cheese   salt and pepper
1½ cans consommé   sherry

Liquidize the cream cheese and 1¼ cans consommé, curry powder,
salt, and pepper until well blended. Pour into individual ramekin
dishes and chill until set. Add some sherry to the remaining consommé—warm through if still jellied, allow to cool, and pour over
the cream cheese mixture. Chill.
    Serves 8.

GAZPACHO

On a hot day thoughts turn to cold soups, and this is one of the best.

2 cloves garlic	6½ tablespoons olive oil
1 green pepper	2 tablespoons vinegar
1 Spanish onion	3 tablespoons red wine
6 large ripe tomatoes	3¾ cups ice water
½ cucumber	pepper

Liquidize the garlic, half the seeded green pepper, half the onion, 4 skinned and seeded tomatoes, half of the half cucumber, oil, vinegar, and wine. Add this to the ice water. Season well with plenty of pepper. Leave to chill.

Chop the remaining green pepper, onion, tomatoes, and cucumber very finely indeed and put them in separate bowls. Your guests then sprinkle spoonfuls of each vegetable into their soup. If you can be bothered, croutons are always much appreciated.

Serves 6.

ORANGE AND TOMATO SOUP

Surprisingly good, considering package soup is not usually thought of as a gastronomic delicacy.

1 package dehydrated tomato	2½ tablespoons orange liqueur
soup	4 tablespoons cream
1 orange	

Make up the tomato soup with 3¾ cups water. Grate the rind of the orange and add to the soup, together with the juice. Simmer for a few minutes. Just before serving add the liqueur. Put a tablespoon of cream into the bottom of each bowl. Pour on the soup.

Serves 4.

SPINACH SOUP

Definitely for the busy cook.

1 10-ounce package frozen
   spinach, thawed
1¼ cups cream
1 clove garlic, crushed

salt
freshly milled black pepper
2½ tablespoons dry sherry or
   white wine

Mix all the ingredients well together and chill before serving. (Add some milk if too thick.)
Serves 4.

TOMATO CONSOMMÉ

Another delicious summer recipe.

2 envelopes unflavored gelatin
1 chicken bouillon cube
2 cups boiling water
1 19-ounce can tomato juice
1 tablespoon lemon juice
Angostura bitters
seasoning

mint freeze:
   2½ tablespoons finely chopped
   mint
   1 tablespoon lemon juice
   ¾ cup lemon soda
   lemon slices

Dissolve the gelatin and bouillon cube in the boiling water. Add the tomato juice, some lemon juice, and a few drops Angostura bitters. Season well. Leave to set in the fridge.

Meanwhile mix together the mint, lemon juice, and lemon soda. Pour into an ice tray and freeze to the soft-ice stage.

To serve, chop up the tomato jelly and pile into glasses; top with the mint freeze and lemon slices.
Serves 4 to 6.

TOMATO SOUP

It is much nicer than commercial tomato soup.

1 large onion	6 cups good stock
2 pounds tomatoes	pinch of thyme
3 tablespoons butter	salt and pepper
4 tablespoons flour	⅔ cup heavy cream
1 cup white wine	few chopped chives

Peel and chop the onion. Peel and dice the tomatoes, not too small. Melt the butter and cook the onion until golden. Add the flour and stir constantly for about 2 minutes. Remove from the heat and add the wine and stock. Return to the stove and add the rest of the ingredients except the cream and chives. Cover and simmer for about an hour. Liquidize. Reheat before serving in individual bowls with a dollop of cream in the bottom. Sprinkle with chopped chives.

Serves 6.

COQUILLES ST. JACQUES

This is the best recipe that I know for this delicious dish, but unless you have a cheap source of scallops it can be very expensive.

12 bay scallops
2 tablespoons pork drippings or
olive oil
6 shallots or 2 small onions,
finely chopped
¼ pound button mushrooms,
sliced

salt and pepper
¼ bottle dry white wine
⅔ cup heavy cream
2 beaten egg yolks
3 tablespoons bread crumbs
¼ cup grated cheese

Wash the scallops and scrub the shells. Cut each white part into three and reserve the orange. Melt the fat and cook the scallops gently for 10 minutes with the shallots, mushrooms, and salt and pepper. Meanwhile boil the wine until it is reduced by half. Add this to the scallops with the cream, egg yolks, and orange parts of scallops. Simmer gently for about 20 minutes until the mixture thickens. Then spoon it into four or six shells. Sprinkle with bread crumbs and cheese and put under a hot grill until brown.

Serves 4 to 6, depending on your generosity or your guests' hunger.

CRAB DIABLE

Just the thing to impress a mother-in-law who thinks you can't even boil an egg for her darling son. And it's not much harder.

1 small onion
1 shallot
2 tablespoons butter
2 tablespoons brandy
1 tablespoon mustard
1¼ cups white sauce (1½
tablespoons butter and flour,
1¼ cups milk)

1 large can crab meat, drained
and flaked
brown bread crumbs

Sauté the finely chopped onion and shallot in the butter; when golden stir in the brandy and mustard. Make the white sauce, then add the crab meat and onion mixture. Spoon this into scallop shells or ramekins and sprinkle with bread crumbs. Brown under a hot grill and serve immediately.

Serves 4 to 6, depending on the size of the shells.

CRAB MOUSSE

This is a pleasant cold first course, easily made in advance.

5 ounces crab meat, fresh,
    frozen, or canned
1½ tablespoons lemon juice
cayenne pepper
salt and freshly milled black
    pepper
⅔ cup heavy cream

2 eggs
1 envelope unflavored gelatin
4 tablespoons sherry, preferably
    dry
parsley to garnish
lemon slices

Mix together the crab meat, lemon juice, and cayenne. Season lightly. Warm the cream in a saucepan and add the egg yolks one by one. Cook gently, stirring all the time until the mixture thickens. Dissolve the gelatin in the sherry and add to the cream mixture. Allow to cool a bit and then add the crab meat. Beat the egg whites until stiff and fold them into the crab mixture. Pour into individual ramekins and chill until serving. Garnish with a little chopped parsley and lemon slices.

Serves 6.

KIPPER FILLETS MARINATED IN WHITE WINE

All working cooks must have a large repertoire of good recipes that not only can be prepared the night before, but are better for it. This is a classic example.

¼ cup dry white wine
4 tablespoons oil
2 tablespoons lemon juice
1 onion, finely sliced into rings
masses of freshly ground black
  pepper

3 bay leaves
2 7-ounce cans kipper fillets,
  with all black skin peeled off

Mix together the wine, oil, lemon juice, onion, pepper, and bay leaves in a dish. Add the kipper fillets and leave to marinate for at least 24 hours in a cool place. The fillets can be drained or served in the juices together with brown bread and butter.
Serves 6.

MOULES MARINIÈRES

This is one of my most favorite recipes ever but I only prepare it for people I really love. Whatever experts say, washing, scraping, and bearding mussels takes simply hours. So for loved ones . . .

3 quarts mussels
2 tablespoons butter
1 onion or 4 shallots, chopped
1½ cups dry white wine

salt and pepper
sprig of thyme or 1 stalk celery,
  chopped
handful of chopped parsley

Under running water, wash and scrape each mussel and remove the beards. Throw away any that are cracked, open, or in any way damaged. Melt the butter in a large pan and sauté the onion until soft. Add the wine, salt, pepper, and thyme or celery with the mussels. Cover and cook over a high heat for about 5 minutes or until all the mussels have opened. Shake the pan from time to time. Take the mussels out of the pan with a slotted spoon and boil the liquid until it is reduced by half. At the last minute add the parsley, pour the liquid over the mussels, and serve at once. Really loving cooks remove the one half of each shell while the liquid is reducing. As this is only done in the most expensive restaurants, filled with junior chefs with little else to do, it is not a task I have ever considered essential.

Some people add 1 cup of heavy cream with the parsley, but I think it spoils the peasanty taste of the meal.

Serves 6.

SOLE AND MUSSEL FLAN

The rich use sole, but to my taste it's just as good with any decent-quality white fish.

½ pound pastry	small jar of pickled mussels, well
2 shallots or ½ small onion,	rinsed
chopped	⅔ cup dry white wine
4 fillets sole	1¼ cups heavy cream
¼ cup butter	seasoning

Preheat oven to 350° F. Roll out the pastry until fairly thin and line an 8-inch flan dish with it. Cover with greaseproof paper weighted with a few dried beans or peas or something, and bake for about 20 minutes or until golden brown.

Chop the shallots finely and roll up the fillets. Melt the butter and gently sauté the shallots. Then add the fillets, mussels, wine, and cream. Season well. Cook for 10 minutes over a gentle heat and then remove all the fish. Keep warm. Reduce the sauce by half.

Arrange the fish in the hot flan case (warm through again if necessary, as this can be prepared the day before) and pour the sauce on top.

Serves 4 as a main course, 8 as a starter.

BRANDIED SHRIMPS WITH RICE

Expensive first course but more original than boring shrimp cocktail.

¼ pound rice	nutmeg
3 tablespoons butter	2½ tablespoons brandy
⅓ pound cooked, shelled shrimps	1 cup heavy cream
freshly milled pepper	chopped parsley
lemon juice	

Cook the rice and keep warm in the oven. Melt the butter and sauté the shrimps for a few minutes, having seasoned them with the pepper, lemon juice, and nutmeg. Warm the brandy, set alight and pour over the shrimps, shaking the pan well. When the flames have gone out, add the cream and let it boil until it thickens, continuously shaking. Put the rice into individual ramekins and pour the shrimp mixture on top. Sprinkle with parsley.
Serves 4.

WHISKY PRAWNS

First class.

½ pound rice	seasoning
4 tablespoons butter	¼ cup whisky
2 tablespoons olive oil	¼ cup dry white wine
1 small onion, chopped	¼ cup heavy cream
2 cloves garlic, crushed	about 2 teaspoons cornstarch
1 pound prawns	cayenne pepper
2 tomatoes, peeled and seeded	

Cook the rice and keep warm. Melt the butter and oil in a pan and sauté the onion and garlic until soft. Add the prawns and chopped tomatoes, season well, and sauté for a few minutes. Warm half the whisky in a ladle and add to the prawns. Flame, shaking the pan. Pour on the wine and keep on a low heat for about five minutes. Remove the prawns and keep warm. Mix together the remaining whisky, cream, and cornstarch, and add to the sauce. Bring to the boil and add a pinch of cayenne, plus some more seasoning if necessary. Serve on individual warmed dishes—a layer of rice with the prawns on top and the sauce poured over.

Serves 6 to 8.

PRAWN AND ORANGE SALAD

Not a starter you'll have had hundreds of times. Interesting, I think.

¾ pound prawns	juice of ½ lemon
4 oranges	seasoning
3½ tablespoons orange liqueur	sugar
1 small onion, chopped	

Shell the prawns and marinate them in the juice of 1 orange and the liqueur for a couple of hours. Marinate the onion in some lemon juice for about 30 minutes. Slice the remaining oranges and add to the prawns, together with the onion. Season well and add as much sugar as you think necessary (virtually none to my taste). Toss before serving with brown bread and butter.

Serves 6.

SALMON MOUSSE

Tinned salmon is not my favorite food, but the combination of ingredients in this recipe really tastes good.

1 fairly large cucumber	salt and pepper
1 envelope unflavored gelatin	⅔ cup evaporated milk
2 8-ounce cans salmon	a little oil and vinegar dressing
1½ tablespoons sherry	

Cut one quarter off the cucumber and put it in a polythene bag in the fridge. Peel and seed the rest. Boil it in a little water until it is soft and drain it, reserving the water. Dissolve the gelatin in ½ cup of the water. Liquidize the drained salmon, cucumber, gelatin, sherry, salt, and pepper. Whip the evaporated milk until as stiff as possible in a large bowl. Fold the salmon mixture into it. Pour into a wetted mold and leave in the fridge overnight. Turn it out a couple of hours before serving and decorate with the remaining cucumber which has been finely sliced and marinated in oil and vinegar dressing.
Serves 6.

SCALLOPS NEWBURG

A rich beginning to a memorable meal.

2 tablespoons butter	⅔ cup heavy cream
8 cleaned scallops, either bay or	2½ tablespoons sherry
deep sea	salt and cayenne pepper
dash of lemon juice	a little greenery
1 tablespoon flour	

Melt half the butter. Cut the scallops in half and simmer in the butter for a few minutes. Add the lemon juice and simmer for another minute or two. Make a roux out of the remaining butter and the flour, add the cream and bring almost to the boil. Add the sherry, seasoning, scallops, and warm through well, being careful

not to boil. Pour into individual ramekins and garnish with a little greenery. Serve with brown bread and butter.
Serves 4.

SHELLFISH SUMMER

Good.

2 tablespoons butter	1 cup white wine
1 onion, chopped	12 cooked, shelled large shrimps
1 tablespoon tomato purée	¾ pound whole button
salt and freshly ground black	mushrooms
pepper	2 quarts mussels, shelled
1 tablespoon sugar	some lemon juice
1 tablespoon chopped parsley	a little greenery to garnish
1 tablespoon flour	boiled rice

Melt the butter and sauté the onion until golden. Add the tomato purée, salt, pepper, sugar, and parsley. Simmer briefly. Stir in the flour, add the wine and cook for about 15 minutes over a gentle heat. Add the shrimps, mushrooms, and mussels. Cook until tender. Sprinkle with some lemon juice and parsley and serve with rice.
Serves 4 to 6.

SHRIMP AND MUSHROOM APPETIZER

Equally nice as an easy supper dish.

3 tablespoons butter	cayenne pepper or curry powder
½ pound button mushrooms	3½ tablespoons sherry
½ pound shrimps	4 slices plain toast
lemon juice	greenery to garnish

Melt the butter. Slice the mushrooms and put in a saucepan with the shrimps and cook over a low heat for 3 or 4 minutes. Add the rest of the ingredients, stir, and cook until warmed through. Pour onto the hot toast and sprinkle with parsley.
Serves 4.

TUNA RAMEKINS

A remarkably good starter despite the odd mixture of ingredients. Make it in the morning for greater convenience in the evening.

4 eggs	⅔ cup white wine
1 7-ounce can tuna	1 can condensed mushroom soup
1 heaped tablespoon arrowroot	1 large package potato chips

Hard cook the eggs. Drain and flake the tuna. Dissolve the arrowroot in the wine in a large pan. Stir in the soup and heat. Coarsely chop the eggs and add to the pan with the fish. Crush the chips and add half to the mixture. Divide between the ramekins. Allow to cool. Sprinkle the tops with the remaining chips and heat through before serving.

Serves 6 to 8, depending on the size of the ramekins.

(This can also be served in one larger dish, as a main supper course, with a salad.)

Main Courses

BEEF STROGANOFF

Well cooked, this is one of my favorite dishes. For years I cooked it but rarely, believing that it would only work with top quality fillet. My local butcher told me that that simply wasn't true and that any good quality steak would do. Now that the whole process is cheaper I do it more often.

1½ pounds good quality steak	salt, pepper, and paprika
⅓ cup butter	1½ tablespoons brandy
1 small onion, chopped as finely as possible	1½ tablespoons sherry
	⅔ cup sour cream
½ pound button mushrooms, finely sliced	little lemon juice to taste

First remove every scrap of fat and gristle from the steak. Then cut it into as fine strips as you have time for. Meanwhile melt the butter, fry the onion until it is transparent, and then add the mushrooms. When all is cooked remove the vegetables and keep warm. Add a little more butter if necessary and sauté the meat for the minimum possible time (it depends on the size of your strips). Sprinkle fairly lavishly with salt, pepper, and paprika, return the vegetables, and pour in the brandy and sherry. Shake the pan briskly for a moment or two, stir in the cream and a very little lemon juice. Serve with rice or noodles as soon as the cream is hot but not boiling.

Serves 4 to 6.

CHILI CON CARNE

As, strictly speaking, this should be served with beans and rice, it is very filling indeed.

2½ tablespoons oil	1 good tablespoon cornstarch
2 onions, sliced	orégano
3 cloves garlic, chopped	bay leaf
1½ pounds ground beef	pinch of cayenne
½ pound ground pork	pinch of paprika
2½ cups red wine	salt and pepper
2½ tablespoons chili powder	red kidney beans

Heat the oil and sauté the onions and garlic until transparent. Then add the meat and sauté until brown. Pour on the wine and bring to the boil. Dissolve the chili powder in a little water, together with the cornstarch, and add to the casserole. It is difficult to be exact on the quantity of chili powder to use. Find out from your grocer just how strong his particular brand is and use it accordingly. Some palates are a whole lot tougher than others, so know your friends. Add the rest of the seasonings and cook gently, either in the oven or on the stove, until the meat is tender. This should take just over an hour. Serve with red kidney beans. One tin should be enough for 6. Serve rice as well if you have the appetite.

Serves 6 or more.

VERY EASY COTTAGE PIE

I don't like cold meat turned into cottage pie, but made this way with fresh meat it's no work and tastes infinitely better.

1 good tablespoon oil	1 cup sherry or red wine
1 pound ground beef	salt and pepper
1 onion, chopped	mashed potatoes
1 clove garlic, crushed	grated cheese
dash of vinegar	butter
4 tablespoons tomato paste	

Heat the oil and sauté the meat until it is brown. Stir in the onion, and garlic, if you care for it. Cook until the onion is transparent and then stir in the vinegar and the tomato paste. Add the sherry or wine and seasonings, and simmer for about 30 minutes. Keep the meat moist but not runny—by adding either more wine or water or stock.

When cooked put in a casserole, cover with mashed potatoes (instant are acceptable if not sensational), sprinkle with cheese, dot with butter, and bake either in a hot oven for 10 minutes or in a slow oven for 30 minutes.

Serves 4.

VERY EASY LASAGNE

This is made in the same way as Very Easy Cottage Pie and is just as simple.

1 good tablespoon oil	salt and pepper
1 pound ground beef	¾ pound lasagne
1 onion, chopped	1¼ cups strong cheese sauce
1 clove garlic, crushed	(1½ tablespoons butter and
dash of vinegar	flour, 1¼ cups milk, ½ cup
4 tablespoons tomato paste	grated cheese)
1¼ cups sherry or red wine	grated cheese

Heat the oil and sauté the meat until it is brown. Stir in the onion, and garlic, if you care for it. Cook until the onion is transparent and then stir in the vinegar and the tomato paste. Add the sherry or wine and seasonings, and simmer for about 30 minutes. Keep the meat moist and add a little more wine, water, or stock if it gets too dry.

Preheat oven to 300° F. Cook the lasagne according to instructions on the package—probably boil for 15 minutes in salted water. Butter a casserole generously and then layer with lasagne, cheese sauce, and meat mixture; continue until ingredients are used up. End with a cheese sauce layer. Sprinkle thickly with cheese and cook in the oven for 30 minutes.

Serves 8.

You can add extra layers of semicooked carrots, zucchini, or celery if you care to.

VERY EASY MOUSSAKA

This is first cousin to Very Easy Cottage Pie and Very Easy Lasagne but is slightly more trouble, as frying eggplants can be a little tedious.

2 pounds eggplants	4 tablespoons tomato paste
salt	1¼ cups sherry or red wine
at least 4 tablespoons oil	salt and pepper
1 further good tablespoon oil	1¼ cups strong cheese sauce
1 pound ground beef	(1½ tablespoons butter and
1 onion, chopped	flour, 1¼ cups milk, ½ cup
1 clove garlic, crushed	grated cheese
dash of vinegar	optional grated cheese

Finely slice the eggplants and sprinkle them with salt. Leave to sweat for at least 30 minutes. Wipe the salt and water off them with absorbent paper. Heat the oil and fry the eggplants, turning once, until they are brown and transparent. As each lot is cooked, drain well on absorbent paper.

Heat the good tablespoon of oil and sauté the meat until it is brown. Stir in the onion, and garlic, if you care for it. Cook until the onion is transparent and then stir in the vinegar and the tomato paste. Add the sherry or wine and seasonings and simmer for about 30 minutes. Keep the meat moist and add a little more wine, water, or stock if it gets too dry.

Preheat oven to 300° F. Butter a casserole and layer it with all the ingredients, ending with a cheese sauce layer. Sprinkle with grated cheese if you care to. Cover and cook for 30 minutes in the oven, then uncover and cook for a further 30 minutes.

Serves 6 to 8.

Some people prefer a plain béchamel sauce to a cheese sauce; I don't.

SPAGHETTI BOLOGNESE

This lends itself to infinite variations, all good, and is certainly a cheap way of feeding lots of people. Especially useful for feeding friends who help paint your house, dig your garden, or turn out your garage, i.e. it takes a short time to prepare and then cooks happily for some time by itself.

1 good tablespoon olive oil
¼ pound bacon, chopped
2 onions, chopped
1 to 2 cloves garlic (or more), crushed
1 stalk celery, chopped
1 pound ground beef
2½ tablespoons tomato paste
1 5-ounce can tomatoes
1 green pepper, seeded and finely chopped
1¼ cups beef stock (cube does well)
2 cups red or white wine
salt and masses of pepper
little nutmeg
basil, tarragon, thyme, or bay leaves to taste
thickening if desired
spaghetti
grated Parmesan cheese

Heat the olive oil, sauté the bacon, and then add onions, garlic, and celery. When they are lightly browned remove them. Add a little more oil if necessary and fry the meat until it ceases to be at all red. Then stir in the bacon, onion mixture, tomato paste, tomatoes, green pepper, stock, wine, and seasonings that you like. Stir from time to time and simmer for at least an hour, thickening if desired. Cook spaghetti, pour sauce over, and serve, offering grated Parmesan separately.

Serves 6 to 8.

Should more people need to be fed, thicken the sauce with cornstarch and add more wine or stock. Be extra generous with the cheese.

ROAST MEAT WITH A DIFFERENCE

An extremely pleasant way of roasting any meat is to baste it with wine. If the meat, be it beef, lamb, poultry, or cracklingless pork, is fat free, first heat a little oil with herbs, salt, garlic if liked, and a little wine. Pour this over the meat and roast in the usual way. From time to time instead of basting with just the existing pan juices, baste with a tablespoon or so of fresh wine. When the joint is cooked, remove it into a serving dish and skim off all excess fat from the pan juices. Do this by allowing the pan to cool, after which it becomes easy to remove the fat by using a spoon, suction syringe device, or even rolled-up pieces of absorbent paper. Make the sauce by stirring flour or cornstarch into the remaining pan juices, adding another glassful of wine (or more depending on how many you plan to feed) and boiling vigorously. Taste and season as needs must. Stir in some cream just before serving— soured is particularly good. If the joint is fatty omit the oil at the start.

GRILLED STEAK WITH VARIOUS SAUCES

So long as you can afford good steak you need never be without delicious meals. Absolute beginners grill or fry their steaks until they learn how to cook them to suit themselves. The slightly ambitious learn to mash chives, parsley, garlic, or anchovy into butter and put dabs of that on top of cooked steak. The more ambitious cook looks for something more challenging.

Here are five sauces that are easy to prepare, good to eat, and produce something of a connoisseur's delight.

RED WINE SAUCE

1 tablespoon butter	1½ tablespoons sweet sherry,
1 small onion, chopped	port, or Madeira
3 tablespoons flour	1 to 2 cloves garlic, crushed
¼ bottle red wine	dash of tomato purée
1 8-ounce can tomatoes (or 4	bay leaf
peeled, seeded, and chopped	salt and pepper
tomatoes)	

Melt the butter, gently sauté the onion. Stir in the flour for 1 minute. Add the wine. Bring to the boil. Add the rest of the ingredients. Turn down the heat. Cover and simmer for 15 minutes. Remove the bay leaf before serving.
Serves 4.

RICH CHILLED SAUCE

1 cup heavy cream	3 tablespoons mayonnaise
2 tablespoons brandy	dash of lemon juice
½ onion, finely chopped	seasoning
2 tablespoons ketchup	
1½ tablespoons Dijon mustard	
or chopped pickles	

Whip the cream until very stiff and add the rest of the ingredients. Chill until ready to serve.
Serves 4.

MUSHROOM AND BRANDY SAUCE

4 tablespoons butter	4 chicken livers
¼ pound button mushrooms	1 to 2 tablespoons horseradish
dash of lemon juice	sauce
2½ tablespoons brandy	½ cup heavy cream

Melt the butter. Gently sauté the whole mushrooms just until they are no longer raw. Add the lemon juice. Shake the pan vigorously. Pour in the brandy, light it, and shake again. Remove the mushrooms from the pan and keep warm. Meanwhile chop the livers minutely. Sauté in the same pan, adding a little more butter if necessary. When just cooked (don't overdo them) stir in horseradish sauce to suit your taste. Then add mushrooms and cream and warm through. Don't boil.

Serves 4.

BORDELAISE SAUCE

⅔ cup red wine	salt and pepper
1 shallot or ½ small onion, chopped	⅔ cup beef stock
	dash of lemon juice
marjoram	3 to 4 sprigs of parsley, chopped
thyme	2 tablespoons butter
bay leaf	

Simmer the wine with the shallot, herbs, and seasoning. When it has reduced to a half, add the stock. Continue to cook until it has again reduced to a half. Then add the lemon juice and parsley. Strain and add the butter.

Serves 4.

MUSTARD AND WINE SAUCE

2 tablespoons butter	1 good tablespoon Dijon mustard
1 small onion, chopped	handful of chopped parsley
2 cups dry white wine	salt and pepper

Melt the butter and gently sauté the onion until it is transparent. Stir the wine into the mustard until it is smooth, and then pour it into the pan with the parsley, salt, and pepper. Simmer gently for 10 minutes. Either pour the sauce over the steaks or serve it separately.

Serves 4.

BOEUF EN DAUBE À LA MARSEILLES

Another dish that can be made way in advance and heated up at the last minute—the longer it cooks the better it gets.

2 pounds good stewing steak
1¼ cups red wine
3 tablespoons olive oil
ground black pepper
bouquet garni
2 cloves garlic, crushed

¼ pound onions, chopped
¼ pound carrots, chopped
½ pound bacon, chopped
1 14-ounce can tomatoes
12 stoned black olives (though
    green will do)

Cut the steak into bite-size pieces. Put into a large bowl and add the marinade: the wine, oil, black pepper, herbs, garlic, and onions and carrots. Stir and leave overnight in a cool place.

Preheat oven to 250° F. Line the bottom of a 1½-quart casserole with half of the bacon. Then add the meat and marinade, together with the tomatoes. Top with the rest of the bacon. Cover and cook as slowly as your oven will allow for at least 4 hours—ideally 6 or more. Add the olives 30 minutes before serving. If the stew looks fatty, skim off any excess.

Serves 6.

BOEUF EN DAUBE

This is quicker—there is no marinating—but it really isn't quite as good as the previous recipe.

1½ pounds good braising beef
1½ tablespoons olive oil
4 strips bacon, chopped
1 to 2 onions, sliced

1 to 2 cloves garlic, crushed
salt and pepper
bouquet garni
1¼ cups red wine

Preheat oven to 300° F. Cut the beef into bite-size pieces. Heat the oil and add the bacon. When the fat is smoking add the onions and garlic. When they are soft add the meat, plenty of salt and pepper, the bouquet garni, and the wine. Bring to the boil.

Cover and bake for at least 3 hours in a slow oven.

Except for cutting up the meat and waiting for the stew to come to the boil this is fast and it couldn't be simpler. It is an ideal meal to make in the early morning and put in the automatic oven so as to be ready for your return.

Serves 4 to 5.

"LEFTOVER" STEW

This is an excellent way of using up any cold meat. It works equally well with lamb, beef, chicken, ham, or turkey. Particularly turkey. So good is it that it is more than likely that when it appears on December 28 your family won't even recognize the turkey. Hopefully.

4 tablespoons oil	bouquet garni
2 to 3 onions, roughly chopped	bay leaf
1 to 2 cloves garlic, crushed	salt and pepper
1 14-ounce can tomatoes	¼ pound mushrooms
1 tablespoon tomato purée	1 pepper, sliced and seeded
1¼ cups red or white wine	1 8-ounce can corn (optional)
1 pound any cooked meat or suitable mixture, say turkey and ham	

Heat the oil and fry the onion and garlic. When transparent stir in the tomatoes and tomato purée. Pour in the wine and bring to the boil. Add the diced meat and simmer for 30 minutes with the bouquet garni, bay leaf, salt, and pepper. Add the mushrooms and the sliced, seeded pepper and cook for a further 15 minutes. Just before serving you can add a drained can of corn. (N.B. Remove the bouquet garni and bay leaf before serving.)

Serves 4.

BOEUF AU GRAND MARNIER

Extraordinarily good.

1 orange
1½ pounds braising beef
1¼ cups red wine
⅔ cup beef stock
4 crushed juniper berries or
   1 good tablespoon red currant
   jelly
bouquet garni

½ pound onions, sliced
1 to 2 cloves garlic, crushed
salt and pepper
cooking oil
1 good tablespoon flour
2 to 3 tablespoons Grand
   Marnier

Finely peel the orange. Remove white pith from the peel and cut the peel into thin shreds. Store in an airtight container. Squeeze the juice out of the orange.

Remove all fat from the meat and cut into cubes. Marinate the meat overnight in the orange juice, wine, stock, juniper berries, bouquet garni, onions, garlic, salt, and pepper.

Drain, reserving the marinade. Heat oil and fry the meat in it until it is brown. Stir in the flour, add the marinade and orange peel, and bring to the boil. Reduce heat and simmer for 2 hours. Then taste and add more seasoning if necessary. Add the Grand Marnier, cook a few minutes longer, and serve.

Serves 4.

MOTHER-IN-LAW'S HOT POT

So called because it's made with stout and bitter.

2 pounds braising beef
4 onions
4 carrots
2 pounds potatoes
seasoning

equal quantities of stout and
   bitter (about ⅔ cup each) or
   in fact any reasonably dark
   beer

Preheat oven to 350° F. Remove all the fat from the beef and cut the meat into cubes. Slice the onions into fine rings, the carrots into rounds, and the potatoes into slightly thicker rounds. Then pack the meat and vegetables in layers into a casserole ending with a potato layer. Season well. Pour in enough beer to fill two thirds of the casserole. Bake covered for 2 hours—then uncovered for a further 30 minutes. Should the hot pot look as if it might dry out, add more beer.

Serves 6.

BROWN ALE STEW

Perfect for a cold day.

3 tablespoons drippings	1 good tablespoon flour
1½ pounds braising beef	2½ cups brown ale
6 large onions, chopped	seasoning
2 cloves garlic, crushed	slices French bread
1 good tablespoon brown sugar	mustard

Melt the drippings in an iron casserole. Cut the meat into 1-inch cubes and brown quickly in the fat. Remove the meat from the casserole and brown the onions quickly, stirring all the time. Remove any excess fat and replace the meat in the casserole together with the garlic, brown sugar, and flour. Cook for about 3 minutes, stirring constantly, and add the ale. Season. Bring to the boil and cook slowly for a couple of hours.

About 20 minutes before serving, remove any excess fat and pour it over the French bread previously coated with mustard. Put the bread on top of the casserole and put in a hot oven or under the grill for about 15 minutes or until the bread is brown and crisp.

Serves at least 4.

BOEUF EN CROÛTE

This is delicious, easy, and never fails to impress your guests, who always imagine that you must be brilliant. You should use fillet, but, having an enormously reliable butcher who will provide me excellent cheaper alternatives, I never do go to such expense.

2 pound piece of beef for
　roasting
2 tablespoons butter
pepper
¼ pound mushrooms, chopped
2 strips not too fatty bacon,
　chopped

1 onion, chopped
½ cup red wine
½ tablespoon chopped mixed
　herbs, dried or fresh
1 tablespoon chopped parsley
½ pound frozen puff pastry
egg or milk for glazing

Preheat oven to 425° F. Take any fat off the meat and tie the joint into a cylindrical shape. Ideally get your butcher to do it.

Melt the butter, pepper the meat, and fry it in the butter until it is brown all over. Put it in a hot oven for 10 minutes. Allow the meat to cool. Cook the mushrooms, bacon, and onion in the red wine until they are soft, add the herbs, and allow to cool.

Roll the pastry into a rectangle and cut off about a third. Put the drained vegetable mixture into the middle of the larger piece with the meat on top. Fit the pastry around the meat and put the smaller piece on top as lid. Pinch them together, glaze with egg or milk, decorate with bits of pastry if you have the inclination, and bake in a hot oven for 30 minutes more or less, depending on how rare you like your beef. This can be served cold, but to my taste it is infinitely nicer hot.

Serves 4 or more.

BEEF WITH ANCHOVIES AND PORT

This is very subtle.

7 tablespoons cooking oil	12 green olives
4 onions, chopped	¼ cup port
2 pounds good stewing beef	2½ cups good stock
seasoned flour	seasoning
1 can anchovies, drained	a little parsley to garnish

Preheat oven to 325° F. Heat the oil and sauté the onions until golden and put the drained onions into a casserole. Cut the meat into cubes, roll in the seasoned flour, and fry in the oil until the juices are sealed. Add to the casserole plus the chopped anchovies (use kitchen scissors), stoned olives, port, and stock. Season well. Cook covered in a slow oven for about 2½ hours until meat is tender. Garnish with a little parsley before serving.
  Serves 6.

CHEESE FONDUE

A very simple dish to prepare—but it is essential to have a fondue set for serving.

1 clove garlic	3 teaspoons cornstarch per
¼ pound cheese per person	person
(equal quantities Gruyère and	⅛ cup kirsch per person
Emmenthal if possible)	pepper
⅔ cup Fendant, Neuchâtel, or	nutmeg
other dry white wine per	diced bread
person	

Rub a pan with the cut clove of garlic, add the cheese and wine. Cook over medium heat for about 4 minutes. Turn down heat. Mix the cornstarch and kirsch and pour it into the cheese, boil gently, still stirring. Season with pepper and nutmeg. Serve with diced bread for dipping.

WINGED VICTORY

A very simple and yet extremely good recipe for a cozy dinner à deux.

½ onion, finely chopped	rosemary
2 teaspoons chopped thyme	2 bay leaves
salt and freshly milled black pepper	a little butter
1 very young chicken	1 cup dry white wine or cider

Preheat oven to 375° F. Put some of the onion, the thyme and salt and pepper inside the bird, put rosemary under the wings and fit the bay leaves under the wings to look like a victory sign. Season well and cover with dollops of butter. Put the chicken in a baking dish and sprinkle the remaining onion around the edge. Cover with the wine and place in the oven for up to 45 minutes, basting and turning about every 15 minutes. If the wine evaporates, add more.
   Serves 2.

CHICKEN SAN MARCO

I always welcome any chicken recipe that is not in the usual white sauce—and here is one that is quick and easy.

4 chicken joints	1 small can mandarin oranges
seasoned flour	good pinch of tarragon
2½ tablespoons oil	1½ tablespoons orange liqueur
2 cups white sauce (2½ tablespoons each butter and flour, 2 cups chicken stock)	⅛ pound roasted almonds, chopped

Preheat oven to 350° F. Skin the chicken pieces and roll them in the flour. Heat the oil and brown the chicken pieces quickly. Make a white sauce with the roux and chicken stock and add the strained juice from the oranges and the tarragon. Pour over the chicken and cook in a casserole dish for about 45 minutes in the oven. Remove from the oven, add the liqueur and the drained mandarin oranges, and stir to mix well. Sprinkle with the almonds and serve.

Serves 4.

ECHOES OF THE RAJ

Chicken is cheap; brandy and cream aren't, but the finished result is simply produced and tastes superb.

4 tablespoons oil	a few whole peppercorns
4 tablespoons butter	salt
3 large onions, chopped	¼ cup brandy
5 teaspoons curry powder	1 cup heavy cream
1 large jointed chicken	

Heat the oil and butter and sauté the onions, covered, until they are soft. Stir in the curry powder, arrange the chicken on the onions, season, and cover. Cook gently for about 30 minutes, turning the chicken occasionally. Pour in the brandy and cream and cook for a further 5 minutes. Serve at once or keep warm on a very low heat.

If this dish is to be frozen, add the brandy and cream before serving.

Serves 6.

CHICKEN QUARTERS IN SHERRY AND CREAM

This can be made on a gas ring in a one-room apartment and is infinitely preferable to plain fried chicken.

2 chicken quarters	½ pound button mushrooms,
seasoned flour	chopped
4 tablespoons butter	¼ cup sherry) or ½ cup
3 shallots or 1 small onion,	¼ cup white wine) sherry
finely chopped	½ cup cream

Dip the chicken pieces in flour. Heat the butter and fry the chicken for about 15 minutes in a covered pan. Don't let it burn. Remove the chicken and keep warm. Add the shallots and most of the mushrooms to the pan. Fry gently until the shallots are transparent. Then pour off any excess fat. Add the sherry and wine to the pan, scrape up the bits off the bottom, and stir well. Add the cream and heat until it simmers. Season to taste and pour the sauce over the chicken. Garnish with the remaining whole mushrooms and asparagus tips if available.

Serves 2.

If your local greengrocer sells nice cheap mushroom stalks, use them instead, and strain the sauce before pouring it over the chicken.

CHICKEN WITH WHISKY

Very good and much enjoyed.

3 tablespoons butter, softened	4 chicken quarters
1 tablespoon Dijon mustard	1 tablespoon butter
juice of ½ lemon	½ cup whisky
salt and pepper	⅔ cup heavy cream

Work the softened butter, mustard, lemon juice, salt, and pepper into a paste and spread it over the chicken.

Melt the remaining 1 tablespoon butter in a casserole and brown the chicken all over. Cover and cook gently for 30 minutes.

Pour the whisky over the chicken. Allow it to warm for a moment and set it alight. Pour the cream into the casserole and cook gently, without boiling, for 10 minutes.

Serves 4.

CHICKEN QUARTERS IN WHITE WINE AND TARRAGON SAUCE

Another method of cooking boring chicken quarters; can be done even if the cooking facilities are no more sophisticated than a gas ring.

4 chicken quarters	½ bottle white wine
seasoned flour	dash of Tabasco sauce
¼ cup butter	few sprigs tarragon or
3 onions, sliced	1 tablespoon dried tarragon
1 tablespoon tomato purée	sprinkled with a little white
pinch of thyme	wine

Dip the chicken quarters in flour. Melt the butter and brown the chicken gently all over. Add the onions, put a lid on the pan, and leave to simmer for 10 minutes. Stir in the tomato purée and thyme and gradually add the wine. Cover and simmer gently until the chicken is tender (about 30 minutes). Five minutes before serving, stir in Tabasco and tarragon.

Serves 4, or 5 if another piece of chicken is added.

ROAST CHICKEN WITH TARRAGON AND WINE

A variation on the now classic method of roasting chicken with lemon and butter

1 lemon	½ cup dry white wine or sherry
1 chicken	2½ tablespoons heavy cream
½ cup butter	
fresh or dry tarragon (if dry, soak in lemon juice or white wine first)	

Preheat oven to 375° F. Cut a lemon in half and squeeze the juice. Put the 2 halves inside the bird, together with half the butter and the tarragon. Pour the juice inside the bird. Then roast it in the remaining butter for at least 45 minutes, turning from time to time. Put it on a carving dish and keep warm.

Meanwhile pour the wine into the pan and scrape the bits off the bottom. When all is well mixed stir in the cream. Serve the sauce separately.

Serves as many as the bird feeds. If it is large, increase the quantities for the sauce.

BONED CHICKEN IN WINE

Ready-boned chickens are available in some food stores. They are excellent, and though they seem expensive, there is practically no waste. I evolved this recipe when they first appeared on the British market and find that it is much liked. It will take you longer to read than to do.

2 tablespoons olive oil	salt
1 boned chicken (just over 1 pound)	freshly ground black pepper
¼ pound button mushrooms	1 tablespoon cornstarch
1¼ cups dry white wine	2½ tablespoons sour cream

Preheat oven to 400° F. Heat the oil and sauté the chicken in as small a casserole as possible. Keep turning until it is brown all over. Meanwhile peel the mushrooms if necessary but do not slice them. Pack them around the chicken and pour in the wine. Bring to the boil and cook in the oven for 30 to 45 minutes. Then remove the chicken and slice the meat onto a serving dish. Keep warm. Meanwhile boil the sauce vigorously to reduce it by a third. Season it; it may need salt but as the chicken is ready-salted it may not. Sprinkle in some pepper. Mix the cornstarch with the minimum of water and stir it into the sauce. Heat a little longer. Stir in the cream and pour the sauce over the chicken.

Serves 3 to 4.

COQ AU VIN

This simplified version of the French classic is simple to prepare, fairly quick, and can be done a day in advance if need be.

2 tablespoons olive oil	**seasoning**
1 to 2 cloves garlic, crushed	**3 tablespoons oil or butter**
6 small onions	**1 tablespoon butter**
1 chicken, cut into pieces	**2 tablespoons flour**
½ bottle red wine	**¼ pound button mushrooms or**
bouquet garni	**more, peeled**
1 to 2 bay leaves	

Heat the oil and gently sauté the garlic and onions. When they are fairly soft add the giblets and wing tips. When these are brown add the wine, herbs, and seasoning. Bring to the boil and simmer for a couple of hours.

Meanwhile sauté the chicken pieces in either oil or butter. They should be fairly well cooked. Put them in a casserole. Mash the butter and flour together. When the stock is cooked take out the onions and add them to the casserole, together with the mushrooms. Strain the rest of the sauce onto the butter and flour thickening, stir, and pour over the chicken. This can all be done the day or morning before your dinner party.

When you want the *coq au vin,* heat it up in a medium-hot oven (325° F.) for 30 minutes. Don't leave it in too long or the flesh starts coming off the bones, which isn't pretty. The sauce is so good it does need bread, potatoes, or rice to ensure you can eat it all.

Serves 4 to 6, depending on how the chicken has been cut.

CHICKEN IN PORT

Which is a change from coq au vin *and much easier.*

2 tablespoons oil	1 cup port
3 tablespoons butter	seasoning
1 large onion, chopped	a little arrowroot
generous quantity of chopped parsley	fried bread triangles water cress
1 large jointed chicken	

Heat the oil and butter and sauté the onion and parsley in a covered pan. When soft add the chicken and port. Season well. Cover and cook till tender, which should be in 30 minutes. Thicken the sauce with a little arrowroot (or cornstarch) and arrange in a deep serving dish. Garnish with fried bread triangles and water cress.

Serves 6.

ITALIAN CHICKEN LIVER FLAN

A variation on the quiche lorraine theme of which I am very fond. It makes an excellent light supper dish served with a salad.

¼ cup butter	3 eggs
½ pound chicken livers, cleaned and sliced	½ cup heavy cream or evaporated milk
seasoning	1 baked flan case
⅛ pound mushrooms, sliced	Parmesan cheese
¼ cup Marsala	

Preheat oven to 375° F. Melt the butter and sauté the livers until they are delicately pink inside. That's when they stop oozing blood. Be liberal with the salt and pepper. Remove them with a slotted spoon and sauté the mushrooms in the remaining butter. Remove them after 10 minutes. Pour in the Marsala and stir well. Meanwhile beat the eggs and cream. Stir the livers, mushrooms, and pan juices into this mixture. Pour it all into the flan case, sprinkle with Parmesan, and bake until golden (about 20 minutes).
Serves 4.

CHICKEN MOUSSE

An excellent summer dinner dish, particularly delicious with new potatoes or as part of a cold buffet. Little effort.

1 envelope unflavored gelatin	1 pound cooked chicken, diced
⅔ cup chicken stock	(1 medium-size chicken)
⅔ cup white wine	¼ pound ham, diced
1 sliced tomato ⎫ or olives or	⅔ cup heavy or sour cream
1 sliced green ⎬ cucumber	seasoning
pepper ⎭	

Dissolve the gelatin in the chicken stock, add the wine, and chill. Pour a little of the liquid in the bottom of a straight-sided mold and arrange the vegetables in a pretty pattern. Leave to set in the fridge. Mix the chicken, ham, and cream together with seasoning and the remaining liquid and pour on top of the mold. Leave to set in the fridge. Unmold just before serving.
Serves 6.

HAM BRAISED WITH MADEIRA

This is always popular, the sweetness of the Madeira likes the saltness of the ham, which in turn is vastly improved by the spinach. One of my favorites.

2-pound piece of ham	pepper
1 tablespoon oil	2 cups beef stock
4 tablespoons sweet Madeira or	2 packages frozen spinach
sweet sherry	grated nutmeg
2 carrots	salt
1 large onion	½ cup heavy cream
1 stalk celery	arrowroot to thicken
bouquet garni	2 more tablespoons Madeira

Soak the ham overnight if necessary. Heat the oil in a casserole and gently sauté the ham, turning from time to time until all of it has been in contact with the heat. Pour in the Madeira and try to light it—you may not be successful, but not to worry. Remove the ham and add the chopped vegetables. Cover and leave on a low heat for a few minutes. When the vegetables have started to turn transparent replace the ham on top of them, add the bouquet garni, masses of pepper and the stock. Bring to the boil and either simmer for an hour or so or bake in a medium oven (300° F.).

Just before the meat is cooked put the still frozen spinach in a pan on a medium heat. Stir when it becomes possible. When cooked pour out as much of the liquid as possible. Be liberal with the grated nutmeg and add a little salt. Then stir in the cream little by little, getting the spinach to absorb as much as possible. Keep warm.

Remove the ham and slice it fairly thickly. Arrange it on a serving platter on top of the creamed spinach. Keep warm. Strain the pan juices and boil vigorously for a moment or two. Thicken with arrowroot if desired and then add the rest of the Madeira. Pour over the meat and serve.

Serves 4 to 6.

CIDER HAM

An excellent way of cooking ham, told to me by one of my sisters.

1 ham, size depending on how many you want to serve	**enough cider to cover ham**
	1 cup brown sugar
6 peppercorns	**1 tablespoon mustard or to taste**

Soak the ham overnight if it is salty.

Drain it and put it in a large pan with the peppercorns and enough dry cider to cover it. Bring slowly to the boil and then simmer it for 15 minutes to the pound and 15 minutes over. Keep skimming. Remove the ham.

Preheat the oven to 475° F. Cut off the rind and place the ham in a baking dish. Mix the sugar and mustard with enough cider stock to make a stiffish paste. Cook it at the top of a very hot oven for a few minutes until the sugar bubbles and becomes crisp. Then move it to the bottom of the oven for about another 30 minutes. Should the sugar start to burn, turn down the heat a little. Eat hot or cold.

Serves as many as the size of the ham dictates.

Don't throw the rest of the stock away, use it instead of water to make up almost any packet soup, especially a ham one.

HAM IN ASPARAGUS SAUCE

An ideal dish to put in an automatic oven, to be cooked by the time you get home.

2 tablespoons butter or less	2 tablespoons sherry
1 onion, chopped	½ pound cooked ham, diced
1 can condensed cream of	1 can asparagus tips, drained
chicken soup	¾ cup hard cheese, grated

Preheat oven to 375° F. Melt the butter and sauté the onion until transparent. Then stir in the soup and sherry. Put the ham in a small ovenproof casserole, with the asparagus on top. Pour the soup over and sprinkle with the cheese. Bake in a fairly hot oven for 30 minutes. Serve with rice or creamed potatoes.
Serves 4.

HAM STEAKS WITH MUSHROOM AND WINE SAUCE

Make this simple recipe with ham steaks; much more exciting than merely grilled and not much more trouble.

2 tablespoons butter	1¼ cups white wine
4 ham steaks	¼ pound mushrooms, sliced
¼ cup flour	⅔ cup heavy cream

Melt the butter, sauté the steaks until golden brown on both sides. Remove the steaks from the pan and keep warm in a serving dish. Stir flour into butter and cook for 1 minute, then add the wine and boil vigorously until reduced by about a third. Stir in the mushrooms and simmer for 2 to 3 minutes. Stir the cream into the sauce and warm through. Pour over the steaks and serve immediately.
Serves 4.
    This recipe can be used for turkey breasts, only you need a little more butter in which to sauté them.

DREAM HAM

A very good quick supper dish that is easy to prepare and tastes good too.

12 slices cooked ham, soaked in sherry	1 can pimentos, drained
	grated cheese
½ pound mushrooms, sliced	1 cup heavy cream
butter	2 tablespoons chili sauce

Preheat oven to 325° F. Roll the slices of ham and lay them in the bottom of a buttered ovenproof dish. Sauté the mushrooms lightly in butter and lay them on top of the ham. Thinly slice the pimentos, roll them in plenty of cheese, and place on top of the mushrooms. Whip the cream lightly, add the chili sauce, and pour over the ham. Cook in a moderate oven for about 25 minutes.

Rice and salad go very well.

Serves 6.

ORANGE HAM ROLLS

A very simple supper dish. More interesting than sliced cold ham.

a few raisins	2 oranges, peeled and diced
2 tablespoons orange liqueur	6 slices cooked ham
1 8-ounce carton cottage cheese	

Leave the raisins to soak in the liqueur for about 30 minutes and then mix together with the cottage cheese and oranges. Divide the mixture onto the middle of each ham slice and roll up the ham. Serve with a green salad.

Serves 3.

LAMB CUTLETS WITH REFORME SAUCE

This is richer and better than plain grilled cutlets. It's not much effort except that you have to wash two more pans.

8 lamb cutlets or 4 large chops	½ cup flour
seasoned flour	1 tomato, skinned and chopped
1 egg, beaten	2½ cups stock (cube will do)
bread crumbs	bouquet garni
¼ cup butter	pepper and salt
1 slice bacon	1 tablespoon red currant or
1 small onion, chopped	apple jelly
1 carrot, chopped	1 tablespoon port

Remove the fat from the cutlets. Dip each one in flour, egg, and then bread crumbs. Keep covered until needed.

Melt the butter, chop the bacon into small pieces, sauté with the onion and carrot. When they are brown, work in the flour and continue cooking for a few minutes. Then stir in the tomato and gradually add the stock, bouquet garni, and seasoning. Cover and simmer for about 45 minutes, by which time the liquid should have reduced considerably. If there is need, skim the sauce and strain into a clean pan. Stir in jelly and port and warm through until the jelly melts.

In a separate pan, fry the cutlets until cooked. (Ideally use deep fat and drain on kitchen paper.) Serve the sauce separately.
Serves 4.

LAMB WITH SOUR CREAM

If your butcher provides boned rolled shoulders of lamb this makes a good dinner party dish quite cheaply.

a little oil or butter	pinch of thyme
1 boned rolled shoulder of lamb	1 cup red wine
2 onions, chopped	3 tablespoons red currant or
2 carrots, chopped	apple jelly
2 stalks celery, chopped	⅔ cup sour cream
2 bay leaves	

Preheat oven to 350° F. Heat the butter or oil in a casserole and quickly brown the meat all over. Remove the meat and add the vegetables. Gently sauté them until they start to turn brown. Remove the casserole from the heat, replace the meat, add the bay leaves and thyme, and pour in the wine. Stew in a moderate oven allowing 30 minutes for each pound of the lamb. When the lamb is cooked put it on a carving dish and keep warm. Strain the wine juices into a separate pan and boil for 5 minutes. Stir in the jelly and cream and allow to warm through. Serve the sauce separately.

Serves 6 using a whole shoulder.

LAMB À LA BOURGUIGNONNE

A delightful lamb casserole—which is rather different from a beef stew.

1 tablespoon olive oil
¼ pound bacon, chopped
1 onion, chopped
1 clove garlic, crushed
1½ pounds good quality stewing
    lamb
a little flour

1 carrot, chopped
1 tablespoon tomato purée
2 cups red wine
a little sugar
salt and pepper
¼ pound mushrooms

Preheat oven to 325° F. Heat the oil and sauté the bacon until cooked. Remove with a slotted spoon and sauté the onion and garlic. Remove all fat from the lamb and cut into bite-size cubes. Sprinkle with flour and add the vegetables with the chopped carrot. Sauté, turning often, until the meat is brown. Add the cooked bacon. Then stir in the tomato purée, pour on the wine, and season with a little sugar, salt, and pepper. Bring to the boil and cook in the oven for 1½ hours. Thirty minutes before serving, add the mushrooms, chopped if large, whole if button. (You can, if you want to, leave the casserole unattended for the cooking time, putting the mushrooms in at the start, but I like them not to get soggy, so put mine in later.)
    Serves 4.

LAMB CHOPS WITH PROVENÇALE SAUCE

In this case, the sauce is mostly chopped tomatoes and constitutes a second vegetable.

4 lamb chops or 8 noisettes if
    you can get them
cooking oil if necessary
3 tablespoons olive oil
1 large onion, chopped
2 cloves garlic (or less), crushed

1 pound tomatoes
1 tablespoon tomato purée
salt and pepper
⅔ cup dry white wine
few sprigs of chopped parsley

Grill the chops or pan fry the noisettes.

Make the sauce by heating the oil and gently sautéing the onion and garlic. Do not allow to brown. Meanwhile skin the tomatoes (by dipping in boiling water) and chop them into fairly small pieces. Do this in a bowl so as not to lose the tomato juice. Add them, with the tomato purée, seasonings, and wine to the pan. Bring to the boil and cook over none too low a heat for about 10 minutes. Arrange the chops in the middle of a serving dish surrounded by the tomatoes. Sprinkle with parsley.

Serves 4.

LAMB CHOPS WITH GOOSEBERRY SAUCE

This sauce makes a change from the endless red currant jelly alternating with mint sauce. It tastes good too.

8 small lamb cutlets or 4 large chops	1 pound gooseberries
	seasoning
2 tablespoons cider or sweet vermouth	1 tablespoon sugar
	nutmeg if liked
2 tablespoons butter	

Trim off as much fat as possible from the chops. Place under a hot grill for a couple of minutes each side, then turn down heat and cook gently until cooked through.

Meanwhile heat the cider and butter and add the washed gooseberries. When soft and mushy, liquidize and sieve. Season. Then add the sugar and nutmeg to taste—don't make the sauce too sweet. Serve either hot or cold.

It'll keep in an airtight jar in the fridge for several days, so you could save time and make extra quantities during the gooseberry season. This can also be made by draining the liquid off canned gooseberries, heating them with a little cider or sweet vermouth, and then sieving them, but don't add any sugar.

Serves 4.

LAMB SHASLIK

No sheep's eyes in this—suitable for the most refined Western palate.

1 pound lamb (from the leg or shoulder)	2½ tablespoons wine seasoning
1 small onion, sliced	6 to 8 small tomatoes
lemon juice	6 to 8 small mushrooms

Trim the fat from the meat and cut the meat into small cubes. Marinate the meat overnight with onion, lemon juice, wine, and seasoning. Put the meat on skewers, alternating the tomatoes and mushrooms. Grill. Serve on the skewers on a bed of savory rice.
  Serves 3.

DEVILED KIDNEYS

Even those of us who ordinarily don't like kidneys will like this.

18 lamb's kidneys	1 miniature bottle apricot brandy
12 dried prunes	2½ cups meat stock
seasoned flour	seasoning
½ cup butter	

Preheat oven to 350° F. Trim the kidneys, removing the white core and outer skin. Cut into pieces. Stone the prunes (there is no need to soak them). Roll the kidneys in the seasoned flour and sauté in half the butter for about 7 minutes. Pour over the apricot brandy and flame. Add the stock and simmer for about 10 minutes. While the kidneys are simmering, sauté the prunes in the rest of the butter separately until they are just tender—about 7 minutes. Transfer both the prunes and the kidneys to a casserole dish to-

gether with the liquid and season well. Cook for about 15 minutes in the oven. As this dish is quite sweet, I suggest you serve it with rice and a plain green salad.
Serves 6.

LIVER WITH MUSTARD AND COINTREAU

A most successful way of making liver absolutely scrummy—it is very important, however, that the liver is not overcooked, and it should be served immediately.

4 slices liver
seasoned flour
2½ tablespoons oil
2½ tablespoons Dijon mustard
1½ tablespoons finely chopped onion or shallot
2½ tablespoons finely chopped parsley

1½ tablespoons Cointreau
fresh white bread crumbs
4 tablespoons melted butter
orange slices and water cress to garnish

Roll the liver slices in seasoned flour and sauté in the hot oil for about 1 minute each side. Remove. Mix the mustard, onion, and parsley, and add enough Cointreau to make it a creamy mixture. Spread the mixture onto the liver slices and coat with bread crumbs; press these on firmly. Put the slices under the grill coated with half the butter and leave for a couple of minutes, and then turn them and recoat them with the remaining butter—until brown on both sides.

Top each piece with a thin orange slice, then place under the grill for a few seconds. Garnish with water cress before serving.
Serves 4.

LEMON LIVER

This is my favorite way of cooking liver as the combination of lemon and wine removes all the livery taste. Delicious and takes no time at all to prepare.

1 tablespoon oil	bay leaf
1 pound liver, diced	thyme
1 heaped tablespoon flour	salt and pepper
⅔ cup white wine	4 strips bacon, not too fatty, cut
¼ pound mushrooms	in small pieces
rind and juice of ½ lemon	

Preheat oven to 325° F. Heat the oil and sauté the liver until sealed. Stir in the flour and cook for a moment or two longer. Gradually add the wine and then all the other ingredients except the bacon. Bring to the boil and then cook in a slow oven for 1 hour. Just before serving, fry the bacon, cut up into small pieces, until cooked but not crisp. Add to the casserole, remove bay leaf, and serve.
Serves 4.

PORK CHOPS WITH WINEY PRUNES

Excellent.

12 prunes	2 tablespoons butter
⅔ cup white wine	1 tablespoon oil
4 large pork chops or pork fillets	1 tablespoon red currant jelly
seasoned flour	½ cup heavy cream

Simmer the prunes in half the wine for about 30 minutes. Keep warm. Flatten the chops, bone them if you wish, and coat in seasoned flour. Melt the butter with the oil, fry the chops until brown on each side (about 5 minutes). Then add the rest of the wine, cover, and simmer until the meat is cooked; this should take a further 20 minutes. Remove the meat and arrange on a serving dish with the prunes. Keep warm. Add the wine from the prunes to the pan and boil until reduced by half. Then stir in the red currant jelly and the cream. Boil until the sauce thickens, then pour it over the meat and prunes.

Serves 4.

ROAST PORK WITH ORANGE SAUCE

Which makes an interesting change from apple sauce.

1 5-pound roast of pork	1 tablespoon oil
1 to 2 cloves garlic, crushed	1¼ cups chicken stock
a little chopped parsley	3 oranges
marjoram	⅔ cup white wine
rosemary	
salt and freshly milled black pepper	

Preheat oven to 400° F. Remove most of the fat from the pork. Mix together the garlic, parsley, marjoram, rosemary, salt, and pepper, and rub this mixture into the joint. Heat the oil in a baking tin and add the pork. Roast in a fairly hot oven for about 15 minutes. Pour over the chicken stock and roast in a very slow oven (250° F.) for almost 3 hours, basting from time to time. During the last 15 minutes of the roasting, add the juice of 1 orange and the wine.

Finely slice the other two oranges and blanch briefly in boiling water. Spread them around the joint for the last few minutes of roasting time.

To serve, decorate the pork with the sliced oranges and hand the sauce around separately. If the meat has oozed too much fat, skim it off before serving.

Serves 6 to 8.

PORK CHOPS WITH PIQUANT SAUCE

This is remarkably good and easy; if made the evening before it heats up happily.

4 pork chops	¾ cup water
2 tablespoons butter	1 teaspoon strong red vinegar
4 onions, sliced	1 tablespoon sharp pickle relish
salt and pepper	2½ tablespoons Madeira
1 good tablespoon flour	

Remove all excess fat from the chops. Heat the butter and brown the chops on both sides. Add the onions and continue to cook until they are transparent. Remove the chops to a warm place. Season. Stir in the flour and keep cooking until it browns. Then work in the water, vinegar, and relish. Cook gently for 5 minutes. Taste. It should be sharp; if not, add a little more relish or whatever you have of that ilk in your cupboard. Then return the chops and either simmer for a further 15 minutes or cook in a moderate oven (300° F.) for a similar period. Just before serving stir in the Madeira.

Serves 4.

CHOPS WITH CREAMED CARROTS

This is easy, takes very little time to make, and can in fact be prepared the day before. Just heat it when needed.

4 pork chops (or lamb chops if preferred)	salt and pepper
½ cup butter	2 tablespoons sweet sherry or Madeira
2 15-ounce cans carrots or just under 2 pounds cooked carrots, warmed	3 tablespoons heavy cream plus another tablespoon

Preheat oven to 350° F. Trim all excess fat off chops. Melt the butter and fry the chops gently until they are brown on both sides.

Drain the carrots really thoroughly. Mash them with a fork with salt and pepper. Heat the sherry and 3 tablespoons of cream to boiling point and then beat into the mashed carrot.

Pile the carrots into the center of an ovenproof dish. Making an indentation on the top with the back of a spoon, pour the last tablespoon of cream into this. Arrange the chops around the carrots and cover. Bake for 30 minutes, covered.

Serves 4.

CHOPS BAKED WITH NUTS AND VEGETABLES

If you want to prepare this foolproof dish in advance, work through the recipe until the cooking in the oven stage. It can happily be made the night before and heated for an hour when needed.

2 tablespoons butter	4 tablespoons salted peanuts
4 pork chops	1 14-ounce can tomatoes
2 small onions	seasoning
4 stalks celery	½ bottle white wine

Preheat oven to 350° F. Melt the butter and gently fry the chops until they are golden on both sides.

Slice the onions as finely as you can. Scrape and chop the celery equally fine. Mix the onions, celery, and nuts into the tomatoes, and try to break up the tomatoes.

Put half the mixture into a casserole, place the chops on top, add the rest of the mixture. Season well and pour the wine over the lot.

Put the lid on the casserole and bake for about an hour.

Serves 4.

PORK CHOPS WITH WINEY CABBAGE

This is extremely good.

1 small white cabbage	⅔ cup white wine
⅔ cup heavy cream or yoghurt	pinch of caraway seeds
salt and pepper	grated Parmesan cheese
4 pork chops	dabs of butter
2 tablespoons butter	

Preheat oven to 350° F. Slice the cabbage finely and boil in salted water for 5 minutes. Drain and return to pan with the cream, salt, and pepper. Simmer for 30 minutes. Meanwhile trim excess fat off the chops. Melt the butter and fry chops until golden on both sides. Remove the chops from pan, add the wine and caraway seeds, and cook for a couple of minutes. When the cabbage is cooked add the wine juices. Put half the cabbage in a casserole, lay the chops on top, and spread with the remaining cabbage. Sprinkle with grated Parmesan and dot with butter. Bake for 30 minutes.
Serves 4.

PORK MARENGO

This is not complicated, can be prepared in advance, and should traditionally be served with rice.

1¼ pounds boneless pork chops or fillet	⅔ cup white wine
1 tablespoon olive oil	1 8-ounce can tomatoes
2 medium onions	bay leaf
1 tablespoon flour	salt and pepper
	1 teaspoon sugar

Preheat oven to 325° F. Remove the fat from the chops and cut the meat into cubes. Heat the olive oil in a flameproof pan and gently sauté the meat until it is golden all over. Chop the onions. Remove the meat from the pan, add the onions, and sauté until they are transparent. Work in the flour, and after a minute add the wine. When this is hot, add the tomatoes, bay leaf, salt, pepper, and sugar. Bring to the boil, stirring all the time. Then put the meat back into the pan, cover and cook in the oven for an hour.

Serves 4.

PORK CHOPS WITH RAISINS

Another dish that can be prepared in advance.

4 pork chops	⅓ cup raisins
½ cup butter	2 peeled, cored, and sliced
1 tablespoon flour	apples
juice and grated rind of 1 lemon	salt, pepper, and nutmeg
1¼ cups sherry, Madeira, or	
cider	

Preheat oven to 350° F. Remove excess fat from the chops. Heat the butter in a pan and gently fry the chops until golden brown. Put them into a casserole. Meanwhile stir the flour into the remaining butter in the pan. When this has been worked in and all the bits taken up, add the lemon and wine. Cook until boiling, then add the fruit and seasoning. Pour the sauce over the chops and bake for 1 hour.

Serves 4.

HUNGARIAN PORK FILLET

This is not extravagant—although many people are under the false impression that it is—and the meat is so tender.

1 small onion	½ cup white wine or sherry
2 tablespoons butter	1 tablespoon flour
2 pork fillets (about ½ to ¾ pound each) or boneless chops, diced	¼ pound mushrooms, sliced
	⅔ cup good chicken stock or 1 can consommé
seasoning	⅔ cup sour cream or yoghurt
juice of ½ lemon	paprika

Chop the onion finely. Place in a deep frying pan with the butter and cook slowly until just coloring. Put in the fillets, increase the heat slightly, and brown on all sides. Season, add the lemon juice and wine, cover the pan, and cook for 15 minutes. Take out the pork, skim off the butter, and mix with the flour. Return to the pan and stir until boiling. Add the mushrooms and the stock and simmer for 5 minutes. Meanwhile slice the fillets of pork and return them to the pan with the sour cream and sprinkle with paprika. Heat carefully and then serve with vegetables.
Serves 6.

PORK CHOPS WITH ORANGE SAUCE

This has a light and refreshing flavor.

4 pork chops	½ cup orange juice
1 tablespoon oil	1 teaspoon vinegar
½ orange	pinch of thyme
1 onion	salt and pepper
2 stalks celery	3 tablespoons orange liqueur
1 or 2 crushed cloves garlic	

Preheat oven to 350° F. Brown the chops on both sides in the oil. Arrange them in a lidded fireproof dish with a half slice of orange on each. Chop the vegetables finely, brown them in the frying pan, and spread them on the chops. Mix the orange juice, vinegar, thyme, salt, and pepper together and add orange liqueur. Pour over the chops and cook in the oven for about 45 minutes. Remove the lid and brown for another 15 minutes.

Serves 4.

PORK OR LAMB CHOPS MADE MORE INTERESTING

The only excitement in this is a delicious sauce that can be made practically in the time it takes the chops to grill.

2 tablespoons butter	1 14-ounce can tomatoes
1 medium onion, chopped	½ cup red wine
1 clove garlic, crushed	ground black pepper
¼ cup flour	

Melt the butter, add the onion and garlic. Cook till soft. Add the flour, cook for 1 minute, then add the tomatoes. Stir until they are broken up, then add the wine, and cook a little longer. Make it as garlicky and peppery as you like.

You can put the cooked chops in a bowl and pour the sauce over or you can serve the sauce separately. The sauce keeps well, so it is worth making a double quantity.

Serves 4.

PERNOD PORK IN BREAD CRUMBS

Just the thing for the jaded palate—you'll like it.

4 loin pork chops	**1 cup tomato juice**
1 egg, beaten	**⅔ cup stock**
seasoned bread crumbs	**2 tablespoons Pernod**
2 tablespoons cooking oil	**seasoning**
1½ tablespoons flour	

Remove the bones from the chops and hammer meat well until flattened. Dip in the egg and coat with bread crumbs. Fry the chops in the oil until brown. Keep warm.

Make the sauce by adding flour to the juice, together with the tomato juice and some stock. Reduce, stirring all the time. If it gets too thick add more stock. Just before serving add the liquor, season well, and pour over the chops.

Serves 4.

PERNOD PORK

This is a more simplified version of the previous recipe.

6 pork chops	**2 tablespoons oil**
seasoning	**2 cloves garlic, crushed**
6 tablespoons Pernod	**⅔ cup stock**

Marinate the chops, well seasoned, in half the Pernod for about 12 hours. Warm the oil with the garlic and sauté the chops until brown. Heat the stock with the rest of the Pernod. Pour any excess fat off the chops and add the stock. Cover and simmer for about 25 minutes, without burning the chops.

Serves 6.

POT ROASTED VEAL WITH ORANGE AND MUSTARD SAUCE

This is a good dinner-party dish and not particularly tiresome to do. As the meat is cooked in soup, do not add salt, there'll be plenty.

1 tablespoon olive oil
1 3-pound roast veal
2 old carrots, roughly chopped
1 can concentrated onion soup
⅓ cup almonds
olive oil
salt
2 tablespoons butter

¼ cup flour
1 teaspoon mild mustard (or more)
rind and juice of 1 orange
2 tablespoons Cointreau or other orange liqueur
⅓ cup heavy cream

Preheat oven to 400° F. to 425° F. Heat the oil in an ovenproof casserole, then sauté the meat until it is brown all over. Add the carrots and the soup, together with half a canful of water. Cover and roast for 2 hours, basting occasionally. At the same time bake the almonds in a fireproof dish with a little olive oil and some salt. Cook till brown (about 30 minutes). I always cook double quantities, as I so like salted almonds.

When the meat is cooked, take it out and carve it fairly thickly. Cover with foil and keep warm. Reduce the roast stock to nearly half by boiling vigorously. In another pan melt the butter, stir in the flour, and gradually add the strained stock. Then add the mustard, orange juice, and finely chopped rind, together with the liqueur. Taste it; I like double quantities of mustard, but see if there is enough to your taste at this stage; if not add more. Stir in the cream. Sprinkle the nuts over the meat and pour the sauce over the lot. This will happily keep warm in a low oven for some time, but it must be covered.

Serves 6 plus.

ROMAN VEAL

Rather glamorous.

4 veal steaks	4 slices cooked ham
2 cloves garlic, crushed	2 tablespoons butter
salt and pepper	1 cup white wine
sage	⅓ cup heavy cream

Pound the veal to make it as thin as possible. Sprinkle with the garlic, seasoning, and a pinch of sage. Fasten a piece of ham on each steak with a toothpick. Melt the butter and sauté the meat until brown. Pour half the wine over the meat. Remove the meat and keep hot. Pour in the rest of the wine and scrape up bits in pan. Stir in the cream, heat through, pour over the meat, and serve at once.
Serves 4.

QUICK AND EASY VEAL

And that really does describe it.

2 large onions	white wine
4 fillets of veal	seasoning
2 cups grated Cheddar cheese	flour

Preheat oven to 350° F. Chop the onions and lay them in the bottom of a fireproof dish. Put a layer of veal on top, and then a layer of grated cheese on top of the veal. Add enough wine to cover the veal, season, and cook in the oven for about 1 hour. Thicken with flour before serving.

Serves 4.

CHILLED VEAL WITH ARTICHOKES

Nice.

6 Jerusalem artichokes	6 tablespoons sherry
3 tablespoons flour	seasoning
2½ cups milk	6 fillets of veal
½ cup butter	1 6-ounce can caponata
1 cup grated mild cheese	(eggplant appetizer)

Peel and slice the artichokes. Boil them in salted water for about 15 minutes. Make a white sauce with flour, milk, and half the butter. Boil for about 2 minutes. Remove from the heat and add the cheese, sherry, and seasoning. Cover the pan and leave to cool. Melt the rest of the butter and sauté the veal for 1 minute on each side. Remove from the pan. Mash together the artichokes and the caponata. Cover the fillets with the mixture, roll them up, and fix with two cocktail sticks. Place them in a serving dish (sticks facing upward), pour the sauce over, and chill until needed.

Serves 6.

VEAL WITH CREAM CHEESE

This recipe is fairly rich, so don't have a heavy starter beforehand.

8 veal escalopes	seasoning
4 slices prosciutto ham	3½ tablespoons heavy cream
1 package cream cheese	flour
2½ tablespoons grated Parmesan cheese	butter
1½ tablespoons finely chopped chives	⅔ cup white wine

Hammer the escalopes until thin. Place a ham slice on 4 of the escalopes. Mix the cream cheese, Parmesan, chives, and seasoning with enough cream to soften. Spread this mixture on top of the ham and then cover with the remaining 4 escalopes. Beat the edges so as to join firmly. Dip the escalopes in flour, melt the butter, and brown the escalopes on both sides. Add the wine and more seasoning, and simmer for about 20 minutes.
Serves 4.

FRENCH ROAST VEAL

This recipe takes a little more effort than most, but is well worth it for a special occasion.

6 tablespoons butter	for garniture:
3- to 4-pound veal roast	2 tablespoons butter
1 carrot, sliced	3 strips lean bacon, chopped
1 medium onion, sliced	12 small shallots or 3 small onions, chopped
1¼ cups white wine	6 baby carrots, sliced
bouquet garni	1 cup consommé
2 bacon strips, chopped	1 tablespoon sugar
salt and pepper	salt and pepper

Preheat oven to 350° F. Melt the butter in a large flameproof casserole. Brown the piece of veal all over. Add the vegetables, wine, bouquet garni, strips of bacon, and seasoning. Cover the casserole and bake for 1½ hours, then uncover and bake for a further ½ hour. Remove the bouquet garni. Slice the roast onto a serving dish, pour the sauce over, and surround it with the garniture made as follows:

Melt the butter and fry the bacon in it. Then add the shallots and fry until transparent, at which stage add the carrots. Fry until the carrots brown, then pour on the consommé, sugar and seasoning. Cover and simmer until the majority of the liquid is absorbed (about ½ hour).

Serves 6 to 8.

VEAL STEW

Put this on at teatime and forget it till dinnertime. Simplicity.

1½ pounds veal	seasoning
2 tablespoons butter	1 to 2 cloves garlic, crushed
¼ cup flour	chopped parsley
½ bottle red wine or more if necessary	1 bay leaf

Cut the veal into 1-inch cubes. Melt the butter in a casserole and sauté the veal until lightly browned. Work the flour into the meat and fat. Add the rest of the ingredients, cover, and simmer for about 2½ hours, being careful not to let the liquid reduce too much. Add more wine if necessary.

Serves 4.

PAUPIETTES DE VEAU

This is a delicious way of serving veal and somewhat different from the more conventional veal sauces. It can easily be prepared in advance but should not be cooked until wanted.

8 veal escalopes	2 tablespoons butter
stuffing:	1 cup white wine
¼ pound sausage meat	a little stock
½ cup crumbled stale bread	⅔ cup heavy cream
soaked in hot milk and	
squeezed dry	
1 egg, beaten	
1½ tablespoons minced	
parsley	
a little black pepper	

Pound the escalopes until thin, and trim. Mix the stuffing and add the scraps from the escalopes to it. Spread the stuffing on the escalopes and roll them up neatly and tie with kitchen thread.

Melt the butter and add the veal birds. Gently sauté them, turning several times, for 30 minutes, being careful not to brown them. Add the wine and braise the veal for about an hour until it is cooked and tender.

Transfer the veal to a heated dish and cut off the threads. Add a little hot stock and cream to the pan and reduce over a hot flame for 2 to 3 minutes. Pour the sauce over the veal.

This dish is excellent served with sautéed whole mushrooms or, alternatively, add ¼ pound chopped mushrooms to the pan before adding the cream.

Serves 8.

WIENER SCHNITZEL WITH WHISKY SAUCE

Which makes an interesting change.

4 veal fillets	4 tablespoons tomato paste
beaten egg and bread crumbs to coat	1 bay leaf
4 tablespoons butter	thyme
1 cup thick white sauce (1 good tablespoon each butter and flour, 1 cup milk)	1 stalk celery, finely chopped
	1 small onion, finely chopped
	salt and pepper
⅔ cup whisky	stuffed green olives, sliced
	a few anchovy fillets for garnish

Dip the veal fillet in egg and bread crumbs. Heat the butter and fry the veal gently until golden brown. To the white sauce, add the whisky, tomato paste, bay leaf, thyme, celery, onion, salt, and pepper. Cook for several minutes and remove the bay leaf. Arrange veal on serving dish, pour the sauce over, and decorate with olives and anchovies. Serve at once.

Serves 4.

ESCALOPES WITH ORANGES

This I really like.

4 tablespoons butter	4 tablespoons orange liqueur
4 veal escalopes	⅓ cup chicken stock
¼ cup flour	seasoning
2 oranges	parsley to garnish

Melt the butter in a large pan and sauté the escalopes until slightly brown on both sides. Take out the escalopes, remove the pan from the heat, and stir in the flour. Add the rind and juice of 1 orange, the liqueur, and the stock. Reheat, replace the veal and season well, cover, and simmer for about 10 minutes. Pour into a serving dish and garnish with parsley and the remaining orange finely sliced.

Serves 4.

VEAL IN VERMOUTH

Even a cook whose only facility is an electric hot plate can manage this triumph.

6 veal escalopes	½ pound button mushrooms
seasoning	3½ tablespoons dry vermouth
flour	⅔ cup heavy cream
4 tablespoons butter	cayenne pepper

Hammer the escalopes until fairly thin. Season well and coat in flour. Melt the butter and sauté the meat on both sides until cooked and tender (do not overcook). Remove and keep warm. Cook the mushrooms in the pan for about 5 minutes, add the vermouth, cream, and cayenne. When hot but not boiling, pour over the veal and serve.

Serves 6.

KIDNEY VEAL CHOPS

Veal chops are not so cheap, so they deserve a little more effort in preparation. It's worth it.

3 tablespoons butter	⅔ cup heavy cream
4 veal chops with kidneys	¼ cup sherry
½ pound button mushrooms	salt and pepper
a little chicken stock	
1 tablespoon arrowroot or cornstarch	

Melt the butter and quickly brown the chops on both sides. Cover and simmer for about 20 minutes, turning them and adding more butter if necessary. Add most of the mushrooms and toss them in the butter for about 5 minutes. Remove the meat and mushrooms and keep warm. Add the stock to the pan, and scrape well in order to remove the goodness from the bottom of the pan. Mix the arrowroot with a little water and add to the stock, together with the cream and sherry. Season. Heat the sauce but do not allow it to boil. Pour over the chops and mushrooms before serving, and garnish with the few remaining mushrooms.

Serves 4.

ELEGANT VEAL CHOPS

Try this for a delicious dinner à deux.

4 tablespoons butter	**6 tablespoons light stock**
1 onion, chopped	**½ cup wine**
2 strips lean bacon, chopped	**salt and pepper**
2 tablespoons butter	**1 egg yolk**
2 veal chops	**a little chopped parsley**

Melt the 4 tablespoons butter and sauté the onion and bacon until golden brown. Add 2 tablespoons butter and the chops and cook slowly until brown, turning occasionally. Remove chops when they are cooked and keep warm. Pour away a little of the fat from the pan and add the stock and the wine. Simmer and season with salt and pepper. Beat the egg yolk. Remove the stock from the heat and gradually add to the egg yolk, stirring constantly. Pour sauce into clean pan and reheat. Add the parsley. Take care not to let it boil. Pour over the chops just before serving.

Serves 2.

MY GRANDMA MATHIESON'S GRANDMA OCKLESTON'S JUGGED HARE

Which is an excellent but rather costly family recipe—port was cheaper in those days. But you can easily substitute red wine for port. Haig, the whisky people, recommend you substitute whisky in any jugged hare recipe, but superb though it sounds I've never felt rich enough to try—perhaps when I've a good supply of duty-free!

2 onions	1 washed jointed hare
marjoram	3 tablespoons oil (or more if the
6 cloves	hare is large)
1 blade mace	2 more onions
nutmeg	more port
peppercorns	a little stock or milk
bay leaves	2½ tablespoons red currant or
juniper berries	apple jelly
2½ tablespoons oil	cornstarch
2½ cups port	

Add first nine ingredients to the port and pour them over the hare. Let it stand in the marinade overnight (in my great-great-grandmother's day they left it in the coolest part of the oven for a shorter time, but overnight in a colder place is more convenient nowadays).

Preheat oven to 300° F. Heat the 3 tablespoons of oil, finely chop the 2 additional onions, and sauté them until they are transparent. Then remove the hare from the marinade, dry the pieces, and fry them in the oil until they are brown. Pour in the marinade and more port (probably another cup) and either a little stock or milk. Bring to the boil. Transfer to a heavy casserole and bake in the oven for 2 hours or more.

Remove the hare pieces and keep them warm. Strain the sauce into a clean pan and stir in the red currant or apple jelly, though my great-great-granny used black currant. Thicken the sauce with a little cornstarch, and if you have any of the blood stir that in.

Keep stirring and cook, without boiling, for several minutes. Then pour it over the meat and serve with rice.

Serves 6 or more, depending on the size of the hare.

DUCK WITH APPLE

This saves the effort of making applesauce but looks as if you went to infinitely more trouble.

1 duck	**⅓ cup Calvados**
apples	**salt and pepper**
lemon juice	

Preheat oven to 400° F. Roast the duck in your usual way but stuff it with peeled and roughly chopped apples. Just before serving, peel and finely slice a few more good eating apples. Put the duck onto a carving dish, surround it with the sliced apples, sprinkled with lemon juice to keep their color, and pour the Calvados over the bird. Light it, carve, and eat.

Serves 3 or more, depending on the size of the bird.

DUCK WITH ORANGE SAUCE

Duck is a greasy bird so is always served with a sharp accompaniment to offset the fattiness. When cooking a duck, keep pricking it to release as much of the fat as possible; if need be, cook it longer than traditionalists would advise.

If you haven't the time to make this extremely simple sauce, you should at least cut an orange in two and stuff it into the duck before cooking it. Then serve the duck with cold sliced oranges sprinkled with Cointreau.

1 duck of a size to serve your guests (it doesn't go very far)
2 oranges
1 lemon
1½ tablespoons sugar
2½ tablespoons vinegar
2 oranges, peeled and sliced (optional for garnish)
3 tablespoons brandy or orange liqueur
¼ cup consommé or chicken stock

Preheat oven to 400° F. Roast the duck for about an hour. Keep pricking and basting it.

Peel the 2 oranges and the lemon. Squeeze them and remove the pith from the peel and finely chop the peel. Pour boiling water over it and leave for a few seconds. Strain. Dissolve the sugar in the vinegar and heat until it caramelizes. Then add the juice of the oranges and lemon and the peels. Cook gently for about 5 minutes.

When the duck is done, arrange on a carving dish with the sliced oranges if wanted. Pour all fat off the roasting pan and stir in liquor and consommé. Stir vigorously and get all the bits off the pan. Then add the orange sauce, heat through, and serve. It's excellent.

The sauce is enough for 4.

BOOZY PHEASANT

A glorious dish.

½ cup brandy) or 1 cup sweet   ⅓ cup peeled almonds
½ cup port   )   sherry   salt and pepper
1 pheasant   cornstarch
6 tablespoons butter

Pour the liquor over the bird and leave it to soak in the marinade at least overnight. Cover it. Turn the bird now and then if possible.

Preheat oven to 350° F. Melt the butter in a casserole and sauté the almonds (add a dash of oil to prevent the butter from burning). Remove the nuts and cook the bird until it is brown all over. Replace the nuts, pour in the liquor, and season. Cover and cook in the oven for about an hour (time depending on size of bird). When it is cooked remove the bird and keep warm.

Stir a little cornstarch into the pan juices and bring to the boil. Add a little more liquor or stock if there is not enough liquid.

Serves 2 or 3; it is rarely possible to get a pheasant to feed more.

PHEASANT WITH APPLES AND CREAM

If you are lucky enough ever to get to the stage of being bored with roast pheasant, bread crumbs, and potato chips, this makes an original and very easy alternative.

2 tablespoons butter
1½ tablespoons oil
1 large onion, chopped
1 pheasant
4 tablespoons Calvados or
   brandy
2 cups chicken stock

½ cup heavy cream
½ pound eating apples, peeled
   and sliced
salt and pepper
2 large apples, cored and sliced
   into rings, fried in butter

Preheat oven to 350° F. Heat the butter and oil and sauté the onion until it is transparent. Remove it and sauté the pheasant until it is brown. Do this gently. Replace the onion, remove excess fat if any. Warm the liqueur in a ladle, set fire to it, and pour it over the bird. Then add the stock, cream, ½ pound apples, and seasoning. Cover and bake in the oven for about an hour. Perfectionists carve the bird, arrange it on a dish, strain the sauce, and pour it over the bird. The rest serve the sauce separately. Both decorate the serving dish with apple rings fried in butter.

Serves 2 to 3, depending on the size of the pheasant.

PIGEONS WITH TANGERINES

For country people with access to pigeons, this is the way to make them taste more exciting.

2 onions
6 tablespoons butter
chopped parsley and chervil
4 pigeons' livers, chopped
1 stalk celery, chopped
1½ cups cooked rice
seasoning
4 pigeons

3 tangerines
4 strips fatty bacon
5 tablespoons Grand Marnier
2½ tablespoons brandy
2½ tablespoons consommé or
   chicken stock
1½ teaspoons sugar

Peel the onions and cut in rings. Melt the butter and cook the onions gently. Add the herbs, livers, celery, and rice. Season. Stuff the pigeons with this mixture and a little tangerine rind. Put the bacon over as much of the birds as possible. Brown the pigeons on all sides in butter in an earthenware dish and then flame them with the liquors. Add the consommé or stock and cover and simmer for about 20 minutes. Season. Sprinkle the tangerine quarters with sugar and add to the pigeons and cook for a further 15 minutes.

Serves 4.

TURKEY ROASTED WITH PORT

Superb. Having tasted this, you'll never cook turkey any other way—but it is rich.

stuffing:	sage or parsley
1 can unsweetened chestnut	salt and pepper
purée	1 turkey
1 pound sausage meat	1½ tablespoons oil
⅓ cup port	salt and pepper
1 pound bread crumbs	1¼ cups port
2 eggs, beaten	flour
2 onions, chopped	stock from turkey giblets
1 clove garlic, crushed	⅔ cup cream

Preheat oven to 425° F. Make the stuffing by first mixing the chestnut and sausage meat. Then stir the port into the bread crumbs, and when they have absorbed the wine, mix them into the meat. Add the eggs and other ingredients. Then stuff the bird and sew him up.

Using a pastry brush, coat the bird with oil. Put him in a roasting pan and sprinkle him generously with salt and pepper. Then pour over a little of the port. Cook in a hot oven for 20 minutes, then turn the oven down to 350° F. and cook for a total of 20 minutes per pound. Baste frequently with pan juices, and add more port from time to time. Turn the bird if you believe this is the best way to keep the flesh from drying.

When all is finally cooked, remove the bird and make the sauce by stirring some flour into the pan, scraping everything up, and adding more port and stock made with the giblets. Stir in the cream just before serving.

These quantities would be adequate for an eight- to twelve-pound bird. With a bigger bird you can stuff the other end with something else—say sage and onion—in which case don't put sage into the chestnut and port stuffing. It will be good.

TUNA-STUFFED ZUCCHINI

A fairly cheap, rather unusual dish.

4 large zucchini	**1 good tablespoon chopped**
⅛ pound bread crumbs	**parsley**
¼ cup white wine	**oil**
¼ pound cottage cheese	**lemon quarters for garnish**
1 3¼-ounce can tuna, drained	
and flaked	

Preheat oven to 350° F. Slice the zucchini lengthways and boil in salted water until they are three quarters cooked—the time depends on size and toughness—say 5 minutes. Drain thoroughly and scoop out the seeds. Soak the bread crumbs in the wine and stir in the cottage cheese, tuna, and parsley. Mix well. Stand the zucchini on aluminum foil, stuff them with the tuna mixture, brush with oil, and bake in the oven for about ½ hour. Serve with lemon quarters.

Serves 4.

COD MOUSSE

A very inexpensive dish, particularly suitable for a buffet supper.

2 pounds cod	**1 cup white wine**
salt	**4 generous tablespoons vinegar**
fennel	**1 small cucumber, sliced**
⅔ cup mayonnaise	
1 package lemon-flavored	
gelatin	

Poach the cod in boiling water with a little salt and fennel. Leave until cold, then take off the skin and flake the flesh into a large bowl. Stir in the mayonnaise.

Add just enough boiling water to the gelatin to make it dissolve. When it has cooled, stir in the wine and vinegar.

Peel and slice the cucumber. Pour a little gelatin into the bottom of a mold. Then add a layer of cucumber slices. Leave until set. Stir the rest of the gelatin into the fish mixture, then layer with the cucumber slices, ending with the cucumber. Leave in the fridge overnight. Turn out and serve with mayonnaise and salad.

N.B. This must be made with proper mayonnaise. If you find the taste of the lemon-flavored gelatin too sweet it can easily be made with lemon juice and gelatin.

The quantities are not rigid—much depends on the liquidity of your mayonnaise. Try not to make the mixture too sloppy, but disaster does not ensue if you do.

Serves 4 to 6.

COD BRITTANY

Cod is good and cheap but sadly underrated. You'll enjoy this.

2 tablespoons cooking oil	¼ pound mushrooms
2 pounds fresh cod, boned and skinned	1 teaspoon chopped parsley
	1¼ cups cider
seasoning	1 tablespoon butter
2 shallots	1 teaspoon flour

Preheat oven to 375° F. Grease a baking dish with oil, or butter it if preferred, and lay the fish in it. Season. Chop the shallots and mushrooms and sprinkle over the top with the parsley. Pour over the cider. Blend the butter and flour to a smooth paste and add. Cook the fish in the oven, basting several times, for about ½ hour.

Serves 4.

CIDER HERRINGS

Cheap and good.

4 herrings	chopped chives
seasoning	thyme
1 small onion, chopped	butter
1 apple, chopped	1¼ cups cider
chopped parsley	dash of lemon juice

Preheat oven to 325° F. Remove the bones from the herrings, clean, and lay flat, or ask your fishmonger nicely to do it for you. Season the inside of the fish and sprinkle with onion, apple, parsley, chives, and thyme. Roll up the fish. Butter a fireproof dish well and lay the fish in it. Pour the cider on top and add the lemon juice. Bake for about 45 minutes.

Serves 2 or 4, depending on the size of the herrings and the appetites.

HADDOCK MOUSSE

Delicious for buffet suppers.

2 pounds smoked haddock	¾ cup flour
1¼ cups milk	⅔ cup white wine
1 bay leaf	5 eggs
1 onion, chopped	1 cup heavy cream, lightly
whole black peppercorns	whipped
6 tablespoons butter	

Soak the haddock in cold water for at least 30 minutes. Warm the milk with the bay leaf, onion, and peppercorns, and poach the fish for 5 minutes. Remove the fish onto a flat plate and leave it to cool. Strain the liquid and reserve ⅔ cup of it.

Meanwhile make a sauce with the butter, flour, white wine, and fishy milk. While that is cooling, remove all the skin and bones from the flesh of the fish and then mash it with a fork.

By this time the sauce should be cool. Separate the eggs and beat in the yolks one by one. When the sauce is smooth again stir in the fish. Keep stirring until it is smooth. Then stir in the cream. Whip the egg whites until stiff and fold into fish. Then pour into serving dish and leave to cool. Serve from dish or turn out.

Serves 4 plus.

SHRIMPS IN A SHERRY SAUCE

This really ought to be made with fresh shrimps.

16 jumbo shrimps, uncooked	1¼ cups heavy cream
freshly ground black pepper	cooked rice
salt	cayenne pepper
butter	chopped parsley
⅓ cup sherry	slices of lemon
3 egg yolks	

Cut the shrimps in half lengthways and season well. Melt some butter in a saucepan and toss the shrimps in this. Add the sherry and reduce. When the liquid has almost boiled away, remove from the heat; add the yolks and cream previously mixed together. Stir well and return to a low heat, being careful not to let it boil. When the mixture has thickened, pour it over a bed of cooked rice and sprinkle with cayenne and chopped parsley. Serve with slices of lemon.

Serves 4.

LOBSTER IN CREAM

*Never having met anyone except fishermen and professional chefs
who can watch a lobster being boiled alive, I am afraid that the
only recipe I give is for prepared lobster meat.*

8 tablespoons butter	2 tablespoons warmed brandy
4 pounds lobster meat, sliced	2 egg yolks
seasoning	4 tablespoons sherry
paprika	1 cup heavy cream

Melt the butter and gently sauté the lobster meat with the seasonings for a couple of minutes. Pour on the brandy, set it alight, and
shake the pan until the flame dies. Beat the egg yolks and sherry
into the cream. Pour this over the lobster and warm through until
the sauce thickens. Stir all the time and don't let it boil.
   Serves 4 richly.

MACKEREL NIÇOISE

I do like this.

2 large or 4 smaller mackerel	pinch of saffron (if you can get
2 tablespoons olive oil	it)
2 tablespoons butter	salt and pepper
1 large onion, chopped	½ pound tomatoes
2 cloves garlic, crushed	parsley
⅔ cup dry white wine (cider will	12 stoned black olives
do)	1 sliced lemon
1 tablespoon tomato purée	

Get your fishmonger to clean the mackerel and take out as many
bones as possible. If you have large fish and are using one for two
people, split them down the backbone, which you then remove.
   Heat the oil and butter in a large pan, add the onion and garlic
and cook gently until they are soft. Put the fish on top and cook

for a couple of minutes. Then add the wine, tomato purée, and seasoning, stir, cover, and cook—still gently—for 10 minutes. Take the fish out of the pan and arrange them prettily on a dish. Keep warm.

Reduce the pan juices by boiling vigorously for a couple of minutes. Skin the tomatoes by plunging them briefly into boiling water. Take the pips out and chop them up. Add to the pan and cook gently until the tomatoes are hot. Taste to see if it needs more pepper.

Pour the sauce over the fish, sprinkle with parsley, decorate with olives and lemon.

Serves 4.

MACKEREL WITH GOOSEBERRY SAUCE

Mackerel is a cheap good fish, sadly rather ignored. This is an inexpensive summer supper dish.

1 pound gooseberries	4 small or 2 large mackerel,
2 tablespoons cider	filleted
6 tablespoons butter	seasoned flour
1 tablespoon sugar (or more to	juice of 1 small lemon
taste)	few sprigs of parsley

Wash the gooseberries. Stew them in the cider and 2 tablespoons butter until they are soft. Liquidize and sieve them (if you've no liquidizer, force them through a sieve with a wooden spoon—a tedious process which will soon force you to buy a liquidizer!). Stir in the sugar and warm through until the mixture thickens. This is meant to be tart so don't add too much sugar.

Meanwhile dip the mackerel fillets in seasoned flour. (Unless you arrive at your fishmonger's at the rush hour he will fillet your fish for you; if he won't, change your fishmonger.) Melt the remaining butter in a frying pan. Cook the fish for about 7 minutes, turning once. Remove and keep warm. Continue to heat the butter until it browns, then take off the heat, add the lemon juice and parsley, and pour over the fish. Serve the hot sauce separately.

Serves 4.

SOLE WITH SHRIMPS AND WINE

A likable dish that can be made the day before—just put it under a hot grill when you want it.

8 fillets sole	¼ pound button mushrooms
seasoned flour	1 tablespoon grated Parmesan
butter	cheese
1¼ cups dry white wine	1 small package frozen shrimps
2 shallots or ½ small onion	or 1 small can, drained
⅔ cup heavy cream	

Preheat oven to 350° F. Roll up the fish and coat with seasoned flour. Melt the butter and brown the fish on all sides. Butter a fireproof dish well and place the fish in it. Pour over the wine and bake in the oven for about 20 minutes.

Meanwhile finely chop the shallots and sauté in butter until very soft. Stir in the remains of the seasoned flour and cook for a few seconds more. Pour in the cream and boil for a minute. In another pan cook the mushrooms in the minimum of water or butter. Add them to the sauce together with the cheese, shrimps, and the drained liquid from the cooked fish. Pour the finished sauce over the fish and brown under a hot grill for a few minutes before serving.

Serves 4 as a main course, 8 as a starter.

SOLE WITH VERMOUTH SAUCE

This excellent recipe can be adapted to most fish and can hardly fail.

4 fillets sole, rolled	salt and pepper
12 tablespoons butter	⅔ cup heavy cream
6 tablespoons dry vermouth	few sprigs of parsley, chopped
1 teaspoon tomato purée	

Preheat the oven to 400° F. Butter a casserole. Arrange the fillets in it. Melt the butter and stir in the vermouth, tomato purée, and seasoning. Pour the sauce over the fish and bake for 30 minutes or until the fish flakes when touched with a fork. Add the cream and shake the pan vigorously. Sprinkle with parsley and serve.

Serves 4.

BAKED FILLET OF SOLE

Excellent and easy.

1 tablespoon butter	bread crumbs
1 teaspoon flour	8 fillets sole, rolled
¼ pound mushrooms, finely chopped	grated Swiss cheese
2 shallots, finely chopped	butter
1 teaspoon chopped chives	⅔ cup white wine
1 tablespoon chopped parsley	chicken stock

Preheat oven to 350° F. Cream the butter with the flour and spread on a shallow baking dish. Mix together the mushrooms and shallots, chives and parsley. Spread half this mixture on the baking dish and sprinkle with fine bread crumbs. Arrange the sole on top. Cover the fish with the remaining vegetables. Sprinkle lightly again with a few bread crumbs and a little grated cheese. Dot with butter. Add the wine and a little chicken stock and bake in the oven for about 25 minutes.

Serves 4.

BRAISED SALMON IN WHITE WINE

Makes one long even more for the salmon season.

1 tablespoon butter	sauce:
1 onion	½ pound butter
2- to 3-pound piece of salmon	4 egg yolks
½ bottle dry white wine	lemon juice
salt and pepper	seasoning
bouquet garni	

Preheat oven to 350° F. Butter a large baking dish. Finely slice the onion over the bottom, lay the cleaned salmon on top. Cover with the wine, sprinkle with salt and pepper, and add bouquet garni. Place a buttered piece of greaseproof paper over the fish, cover the dish with foil, and cook in the oven for about 30 minutes.

Remove the skin and place the salmon on a serving dish. Keep warm.

Strain the wine and juices into a fresh pan and boil until reduced by half. Meanwhile, make the sauce: gently melt the butter in another pan. In yet another pan whisk the egg yolks and strained juices over a very low heat, until they thicken. Remove from the heat, whisk in the butter very slowly and add a squeeze of lemon juice. Taste and add more seasoning if necessary. Don't overheat.

Either pour the sauce over the salmon or serve it separately.
Serves 6.

SALMON MOUSSE

And it's great.

1 envelope unflavored gelatin	1¼ cups heavy cream, lightly
2 cups fish or chicken stock	whisked
¾ pound cooked salmon	hard-cooked egg, cucumber,
salt and pepper	green pepper, or tomato to
paprika	decorate
2 good tablespoons sherry	

SCALLOPS IN SHERRY SAUCE

Scallops traditionally are cooked in a sauce and then returned to their shells, in which they are served. If the shells are flat and the contents spill out, serve them in individual ovenproof dishes instead.

6 deep-sea scallops
1¼ cups sweet sherry
1¼ cups water
bouquet garni

1 fillet fresh haddock
1 tablespoon butter
1 tablespoon flour
seasoning

Cut the orange parts away from the scallops. Poach the whites gently in the sherry, water, and bouquet garni for 10 minutes. Then add the chopped orange parts and the haddock and cook for a further 5 minutes. Remove the fish and keep warm. Boil the bouillon vigorously until it is reduced by half.

Meanwhile skin the haddock and slice it; slice the scallops, still keeping warm. Dissolve the butter, stir in the flour and seasoning, cook for 1 minute, and add the reduced, strained bouillon. Divide the fish between four shells and pour sauce over. Keep very hot until required.

Serves 4 as a main course, or 6 (in six shells) as a starter.

This can also be made with white wine, in which case it is much lighter, or with 2½ cups cider omitting the water.

SHRIMPS WITH MUSHROOM AND CREAM SAUCE

This is a perfect dish to produce when you want to do something good in a hurry.

1 pound frozen shrimps, thawed
seasoned flour
4 tablespoons butter
¼ pound perfect button
  mushrooms, sliced

1 cup white wine
⅓ cup heavy cream
few sprigs of parsley, chopped

Dissolve the gelatin in the stock and allow
and mash with a fork or put in an electric m
stir in a third of the gelatin mixture, the sea
Fold in the lightly whisked cream. Pour into a s
the surface with the back of a spoon, and leav
cool. Pour on ¼ inch of gelatin mixture, return to
orate with egg or cucumber or whatever, and co\
maining gelatin mixture. Allow to set.

Serves 4.

SEAFOOD FENNEL

Delicious for fennel fanciers.

6 deep-sea scallops	⅓ pound large shrimps, pee
⅔ cup milk	4 fennel
2 tablespoons butter	⅔ cup sour cream
2 tablespoons flour	bread crumbs
⅔ cup white wine	grated cheese
1 small can crab meat	

Remove the orange part from the scallops and slice the white
parts into two. Poach them in the milk for about 15 minutes. Remove the fish.

Melt the butter, stir in the flour, and, using the fishy milk, make
a béchamel sauce. Add the wine and cook for a little longer.
Meanwhile, drain the crab meat, remove the bones, and flake it.
Add to the sauce with the shrimps and scallops, including orange
parts, and stir well. Keep warm.

Slice the fennel and boil in salted water for about 10 minutes
(the exact time depends upon the size of fennel). When cooked
but not slushy, drain well, toss in butter, and spread on the bottom of a serving dish. Stir the sour cream into the fish and pour it
over the top.

Sprinkle the lot with bread crumbs and grated cheese and pop
under a hot grill for a minute or so.

Serves 6.

Rare beings who don't like fennel can substitute celery, chicory,
or even broccoli.

Dip the shrimps in seasoned flour. Heat the butter. Gently sauté the shrimps for about 10 minutes. (If you are the kind of cook who invariably burns butter, use a little less and add a drop or two of good oil instead; it won't affect the flavor and ought to stop the burning.) Add the mushrooms and the wine and cook for about another 15 minutes. Then add the cream, cook until it is heated through but not boiling. Sprinkle with parsley before serving with plain boiled rice.

Serves 4.

TUNA QUICHE

Quite a substantial supper dish, easily prepared and very good.

½ pound pastry   ½ cup milk
1 7-ounce can tuna fish   dash of medium sherry
1 cup grated hard cheese   freshly ground black pepper
1 egg

Preheat oven to 400° F. Roll out the pastry to line a 6-inch flan dish. Bake for 10 minutes.

Drain the oil off the tuna fish. With a fork flake the tuna in a large bowl and mix it with the grated cheese. Beat the egg with the milk and pour it into the tuna mixture with the sherry and pepper. Stir well. Fill the flan with the tuna and bake for 20 minutes.

You can substitute cream or evaporated milk for the egg and milk mixture but they work out to be more expensive and little better.

Serve this hot with vegetables or cold with salad. Even so, re-warm the quiche for 10 minutes before eating: it's rather nasty straight from the fridge.

Serves 4.

Desserts

FRENCH APPLE OMELET

This is so good that having discovered the recipe I made it three times in four days and still enjoyed it when a friend served it to me, as a great surprise, on the fifth day.

6 eggs	3 tablespoons heavy cream
salt	2 tablespoons Calvados or kirsch
5 tablespoons sugar	2 more tablespoons liquor for
5 tablespoons butter	flaming
2 apples, peeled, cored, and sliced	

Beat the eggs with a pinch of salt and a little of the sugar.

Melt half the butter, add the apples and cook very gently until they are soft. Then add the cream, Calvados, and the rest of the sugar. Keep the mixture warm.

Heat the rest of the butter in a good omelet pan. When hot enough add the eggs and cook. When the omelet is all but done, spread the apple mixture over half of it. Fold it over and slip it out onto a warmed dish, sprinkle with sugar and liquor. Set fire and serve immediately.

Serves 4 to 5.

(You can use cooking apples, but if so add a little more sugar with the cream.)

DELICIOUS APPLE DESSERT

This is ridiculously easy and so good.

2 pounds apples, peeled and sliced	1 tablespoon Calvados
sugar	⅔ cup heavy cream or more
	2 ounces semisweet chocolate

Stew the apples in a little water. When cooked, sweeten to taste (not too much sugar). Then sieve. When cool stir in the Calvados. Pour into a serving dish. Whip the cream until thick, spread over the apple mixture, and then leave in the fridge for several hours.

Just before eating, sprinkle with thickly grated chocolate.

Serves 4 or more.

This can be stretched by lining the serving dish with ladyfingers soaked in Calvados.

APPLES BAKED WITH RUM AND APRICOT JAM

With a family resemblance to everybody's favorite nursery food, apples baked this way are more popular than ever.

8 tablespoons apricot jam	8 large apples
½ cup rum	butter
8 tablespoons raisins	nutmeg

Preheat oven to 400° F. Put the apricot jam, rum, and raisins in a bowl and mix together. Core the apples and wipe them clean. Rub a little butter on them and fill them with the fruit mixture. Sprinkle them with nutmeg and wrap in lightly buttered aluminum foil. Bake on a flat dish for about 20 minutes.

Serves 8.

This can also be made with the runny stuff left at the bottom of the marmalade jar after all the greedy people have eaten the chunky bits.

APPLES STEWED IN CIDER

This is simplicity itself and much nicer than ordinary stewed apples. It's an ideal light dessert at the end of a roast meat and two vegetable meal and can be cooked in the same oven.

 2 pounds apples (cooking or eating)
 brown sugar
 1¼ cups cider

Preheat oven to 350° F. Peel and slice the apples. Put them into a suitable dish. Add brown sugar—quite a lot if you use cooking apples, less if not. Add the cider.

Cover the dish and bake for about ½ hour in the oven. Then baste, uncover, and cook for a further 10 minutes. Serve hot or cold, ideally with heavy cream.

Serves 4 to 6.

TOFFEE APPLE OATS

Rather substantial, rather good.

 8 tablespoons butter
 ½ cup brown sugar
 2½ cups uncooked oatmeal
 1¾ pounds cooking apples

 ⅔ cup heavy cream
 2 tablespoons Calvados
 1½ ounces semisweet chocolate, grated

Melt the butter. Stir in the brown sugar and oatmeal, mixing thoroughly. Leave to cool. Stew the cooking apples until soft, sieve, and allow to cool. Layer the sticky oats and apples as many times as possible, ending with oats. Whip the cream with the Calvados and spread over the top. Decorate with grated chocolate.

Serves 5 to 6.

HOT APRICOT SOUFFLÉ

Not fattening as soufflés go, and not complicated either.

1 28-ounce can apricots	3 egg whites
1 tablespoon kirsch	1 heaping tablespoon sugar

Preheat oven to 350° F. Thoroughly drain the apricots and liquidize them with the kirsch. Whisk the egg whites in a large bowl,
then add the sugar and whisk a little longer. Fold the fruit purée
into the egg whites. Pour into a buttered soufflé dish and immediately bake for 10 minutes or until golden.
Serves 3 to 4.

APRICOTS SWEET AND SOUR

Quite unusual.

1 pound apricots, stoned	⅔ cup sour cream
juice of 1 orange	1 good tablespoon soft brown
2-inch cinnamon stick	sugar
½ cup sugar, or less	1 good tablespoon ground
1 tablespoon brandy or apricot	almonds
liqueur	

Cook the apricots with the orange juice, cinnamon, and sugar until soft. Pour into a small soufflé dish with the liqueur. Cool. Cover
with the sour cream. Mix the brown sugar with the almonds and
sprinkle over the cream. Put under a hot grill until the sugar caramelizes. Chill.
Serves 4.

APRICOT ICE CREAM PUDDING

This can be made well in advance.

1 quart vanilla ice cream (there'll
  be some left over)
3 tablespoons finely chopped
  blanched almonds

1 15-ounce can apricots
3 tablespoons brandy

Let the ice cream soften a little, and then mix in the almonds. Line a 1-quart pudding mold with the ice cream, being careful to cover the bottom and sides well, with two thirds of the mixture. (It may help to put the mold in the freezer for a few minutes halfway through this process if the ice cream is not being co-operative.) Freeze for a few minutes before adding the drained apricots and the brandy. Cover the top with the remaining ice cream and freeze until needed. Turn out and decorate with a few more chopped nuts if required. Serve fast.

Serves 4 to 6.

APRICOT AND ORANGE FOOL

A refreshing, slightly tart dessert of which I am very fond.

1 28-ounce can apricots
3 oranges
1¼ cups heavy cream

3 tablespoons apricot brandy or
  orange liqueur

Gently stew the apricots and oranges for about 30 minutes. Don't let the mixture stick. If there is a lot of juice reserve it. Liquidize the fruit, skins and all. When it is cool stir in enough of the liquid to make the purée like heavy cream. Gently whip the cream (it doesn't want to be stiff), and fold it in with the liqueur. Pour into either a large glass bowl or individual serving dishes.

Serves 6.

BANANA CREAM

A light and refreshing way of serving bananas; dislikers of yoghurt would never detect its existence.

6 medium bananas	sugar to taste
2½ 8-ounce cartons plain yoghurt	3 tablespoons white wine
	1 tablespoon lemon juice

If you have a liquidizer, blend all the ingredients together and turn into serving bowl. Chill.

If you haven't a liquidizer, mash the bananas first and then stir in everything else. Some people decorate this with fine slices of another banana. This must be done at the last minute or it will brown.

Serves 6.

FLAMBÉED BANANAS

Always pleases.

8 bananas	8 tablespoons sugar
¼ cup water	3 tablespoons brandy
1 good tablespoon lemon juice	whipped cream
butter	

Preheat oven to 350° F. Peel the bananas and lay them in a fire-proof dish. Sprinkle with water and lemon juice. Cover each banana with several dots of butter and a tablespoon of sugar. Bake in the oven for about 20 minutes, basting a couple of times. Warm the brandy, light it, and pour over the bananas just before serving. Shake the dish until the flame goes out. Serve with whipped cream.

Serves 4.

EXTRA SPECIAL BLACKBERRY AND APPLE MOUSSE

This I find delicious and refreshing.

1 pound cooking apples	**1 envelope unflavored gelatin**
a little water	**2 egg whites**
½ pound blackberries	**2 tablespoons Calvados**
½ cup sugar	

Wash and peel the apples, cutting into quarters. Put them into a pan with a little water, the washed blackberries, and most of the sugar. Stew gently until the fruit is pulpy. Then liquidize and strain into a large serving dish.

Dissolve the gelatin in a little water and stir it really well into the fruit. When all is cold, whisk the egg whites until stiff and fold into the fruit purée with the remaining sugar and the Calvados. Chill until required.

Serve with cream or not according to your taste.

Serves 6.

CHERRY MERINGUE

Simple, and a nice show off if you have cherry trees.

2 pounds cherries	2 tablespoons cherry brandy
up to 1 cup sugar, depending	2 egg whites
on the tartness of the cherries	½ cup sugar

Preheat oven to 350° F. Wash the cherries and remove stalks and stones. Gently stew them for 5 minutes with the 1 cup of sugar and just enough water to cover. Take the cherries out of the pan and boil the juice until it is reduced by half. Stir in the cherry brandy.

Put the cherries and juice into a soufflé dish. Beat the egg whites until stiff and fold in most of the ½ cup of sugar. Beat again. Spread this meringue mixture over the fruit, sprinkle with the remaining sugar, and bake in the oven for about 10 minutes, until it is a lovely golden brown. I like it hot, but it can be served cold as well.

Serves 4 to 6.

BLACK CHERRY TIPSY TRIFLE

This can't be made too far in advance (say, more than 24 hours) as it gets soggy, but since it takes so little time, it can be made at a moment's notice, though the raisins are better if soaked for a while.

4 tablespoons cherry brandy	2 16-ounce cans black cherries
4 tablespoons raisins	4 tablespoons almonds, chopped
2 packages dessert sponges (for	1¼ cups heavy cream
a wide open dish, or 1 if a	
soufflé dish is used)	

Pour the cherry brandy over the raisins and leave in a jar for several hours. Slice the sponges lengthwise and line a large bowl with them. Strain the cherries, keeping the juice. Sprinkle the cakes with less than half the juice—do not make the cakes too soggy. Spread the cherries over the cake, leaving out a few to decorate the trifle. Add the raisins in brandy and almonds. Whip the cream until nearly stiff. Spread over the pudding. Leave in the fridge for at least 1 hour. (If the pudding is made the day before, add cream before serving.) Decorate with the remaining cherries.

Serves 6 to 8.

CHERRY WINE DELIGHT

A lovely light round off to a good dinner.

1½ pounds black cherries	2 tablespoons red currant jelly
1½ cups red wine	1¼ cups heavy cream
cinnamon	1½ tablespoons brandy
2 cloves	1 tablespoon sugar
5 tablespoons sugar	

Wash the cherries and remove the stones and stalks. Stew them until soft with the wine, a good pinch of cinnamon, the cloves, and the 5 tablespoons of sugar. Remove the cherries and put them in the serving dish to cool. Boil the juice until reduced and fairly thick. Remove the cloves and stir in the red currant jelly. Pour over the fruit. Set aside to cool. Whip the cream with the brandy and sugar and pile on top of the cherries.

Serves 4.

CHESTNUT CHOCOLATE

Good, rich, and much admired, also extremely easy to make.

6 tablespoons butter	3 tablespoons rum or brandy
6 good tablespoons sugar	1 cup heavy cream
6 ounces semisweet chocolate	
1 15½-ounce can unflavored,	
unsweetened chestnut purée	

Beat the butter, add the sugar little by little, and continue beating until at least a little lighter than when you started. Meanwhile melt the chocolate in the minimum of water. Beat with a wooden spoon until all lumps disappear. Allow to cool.

Beat the chestnut purée into the butter cream, stir in the rum or brandy and the cooled chocolate. Butter a loaf tin and pour the mixture in. Leave in the fridge overnight. Turn out. Slice and serve with dollops of thick cream.

Serves 8, or even more if previous courses have been filling.

CHESTNUT CREAM

The oranges are a terrific asset to the flavor.

oranges (number depending on	confectioners' sugar
size of dish)	2 egg whites
1¼ cups heavy cream	chopped nuts
2 tablespoons brandy	
1 15½-ounce can unsweetened	
chestnut purée	

Line the whole of a glass dish with thin slices of orange (cut across the fruit). Whip the cream with the brandy and stir in the chestnut purée, adding the confectioners' sugar to taste. Whisk the egg whites until stiff and fold into the chestnut mixture. Pour this into the glass dish and decorate with slices of orange on top. Sprinkle with chopped nuts and chill.

Serves 6 to 8—it's rich.

FLAMBÉED FIGS

A very light dessert to end off a substantial meal.

12 ripe figs	**3 tablespoons brandy**
3 tablespoons orange liqueur	**1¼ cups heavy cream, whipped**

Carefully peel the figs and prick: they must stay whole. Arrange them in a fireproof dish. Warm the orange liqueur and brandy in a ladle over a flame and then pour them over the figs. Set the liquor alight and gently shake the dish until the flame goes out. Serve at once with whipped cream.
Serves 6.

FRUIT POSSET

If you ever need to make a very good sweet in a hurry, this one can get you out of a difficult hole—providing you have a good store cupboard and can lay hands on cream.

1 8-ounce can soft fruit, i.e.	**1¼ cups heavy cream**
strawberries, loganberries,	**1 tablespoon kirsch**
gooseberries, etc.	**chopped nuts for decoration**

Sieve the fruit and mash it with a fork. Whip the cream until only fairly thick. Stir in the fruit and liqueur and put in the freezer for 30 minutes or so. Take out and put in the fridge at the beginning of the meal so that it is not too hard by the time you need it. Sprinkle with chopped nuts before serving.
Serves 3 to 4.
This has endless permutations: match the fruit to the liqueur, use fresh fruit in summer, use sweet port with loganberries. At a pinch you can just about get away with canned cream, but I would use a little more liqueur to mask the taste.

INSTANT FRUIT MOUSSE

No trouble, no effort, and tastes remarkably good.

1 16-ounce can strawberries	**3 tablespoons kirsch**
1 package strawberry-flavored	**⅔ cup heavy cream**
gelatin	**1 tablespoon walnuts, finely**
1 can evaporated milk	**chopped**

Strain the fruit, reserving the juice. Melt the gelatin in the fruit juice. Whip the milk until it is frothy. Mash the fruit with a fork and whip that in as well. Stir in the gelatin and the kirsch. Mix well. Pour into a serving bowl and leave in a cool place to set.

Then whip the cream until thick and spread over the top of the dessert. Decorate with finely chopped walnuts.

Serves 6 to 8.

This can equally be made with raspberries, raspberry-flavored gelatin and kirsch; 2 cans of mandarin oranges, tangerine-flavored gelatin, and Cointreau; or plums, lemon-flavored gelatin, and sherry.

FRUIT SALAD

There are no laws for fruit salads. You put into them whatever is in season and you like. Mine never have bananas. If you put the juice of the first lemon into the bowl in which you are making the salad, and toss apples, etc., as you chop them up, they won't go brown.

2 lemons	**3 oranges**
2 tablespoons sugar, or more if	**3 apples**
you are sweet-toothed	**2 pears**
⅔ cup water	**2 tablespoons Cointreau**

Grate the rind of the lemons into a pan. Squeeze the lemons, dividing the juice between the pan and the bowl in which you are preparing the salad. Add the sugar, water, and juice of 1 orange to the pan and boil gently for 5 minutes. Peel and finely slice the rest of the fruit and toss in the lemon juice in the bowl. Add the strained syrup and the liqueur.

Serves 4.

The variations are enormous. Kirsch is good especially with pineapple. Crème de menthe is excellent with apples, and any exotic fruit liqueur goes with its own fruit.

NORWEGIAN FRUIT SALAD

It's nice.

12 oranges
12 apples
1 pineapple
1 cup chopped walnuts

sugar to taste
juice of a further 6 oranges
1 cup dry sherry

Slice and peel the oranges. Core the apples, but do not peel, and cut into thin slices. (Both of these should be sliced the width of the fruit.) Cut the pineapple into manageable pieces.

Put the fruit into a bowl together with the nuts and sugar, and add the juice of the other oranges. Chill. Just before serving add the sherry.

Serve with ladyfingers.

Serves up to 12.

SHERBET AND CHAMPAGNE FRUIT CUP

An extravagant, mouth-watering dessert for very special occasions.

enough fresh, diced, mixed fruit
  for 8 people, such as pineapple,
  apples, bananas, strawberries,
  oranges, and seedless grapes
4 tablespoons sugar

3 tablespoons kirsch
1 tablespoon lemon sherbet per
  person
8 sprigs of mint
½ bottle chilled champagne

Fill individual glasses with the fresh fruit. Sprinkle with the sugar and kirsch. Chill. Add a dollop of lemon sherbet and a sprig of mint to each glass.

At the table, open the champagne and pour over the fruit (drink any remains!).

Serves 8.

GRAPEFRUIT CHEESECAKE

The grapefruit gives this otherwise rather rich cake a very refreshing flavor.

1 10-ounce package graham
  crackers
nutmeg
cinnamon
¾ cup butter
2 grapefruit
2 eggs
½ cup sugar
salt

⅓ cup grapefruit juice
1 teaspoon unflavored gelatin
1½ 8-ounce packages cream
  cheese
½ teaspoon each of grated lemon
  rind and grapefruit rind
1 tablespoon lemon juice
1 tablespoon kirsch or more
⅔ cup heavy cream

Either crush the crackers with a wooden spoon or put in a blender. Add a good pinch of both spices. Melt the butter and mix in the cracker crumbs. Press the mixture around the sides and bottom of an 8-inch tin or glass dish. Chill.

Peel the grapefruit and skin the sections, reserving the juice. Keep about six pieces for decorating the top. Cut the rest into small pieces.

Separate one egg and put aside the white. In a double saucepan beat the yolk and the other whole egg, sugar, salt, and 1 tablespoon of grapefruit juice. Stir over gentle heat until it thickens. Cool.

Dissolve the gelatin in a little water and add to the custard. Cool.

Blend the cream cheese with the remaining grapefruit juice, fruit rinds, lemon juice, and kirsch. Gradually beat into the custard.

Fold the cut-up grapefruit segments into the stiffly whipped cream and the stiffly whipped egg white. Mix with the custard. Pour the mixture into the cracker case and decorate with the whole grapefruit segments on top. Chill.

Serves 8.

COLD LEMON SOUFFLÉ

The only word of caution to heed in making cold soufflés is to mix the gelatin really thoroughly into the cream mixture. If this isn't done the consistency is wrong and whole thing is spoiled. It's not hard, just takes persistence.

3 eggs	1¼ cups heavy cream
1 cup sugar	toasted coconut or finely
2 large lemons	chopped almonds
1 envelope unflavored gelatin	
2 tablespoons Cointreau or Grand Marnier	

First wrap some aluminum foil around the soufflé dish—it must stand up at least 2 inches above the top of the dish. Tie it on with string.

Separate the eggs. In a large mixing bowl whisk the yolks, sugar, grated rind and juice of the lemons until they are pale yellow and thick.

Soften the gelatin in the liqueur and warm it gently until it dissolves completely. Thoroughly mix the gelatin into the lemon mixture. Then whisk the cream until it thickens, the egg whites until they are stiff, and fold them both into the lemon. When this begins to set (which will be very soon) pour the whole lot into the prepared soufflé dish. Chill. Before serving peel off the foil and decorate the sides and top with the coconut or nuts.

Serves 6.

LEMON SYLLABUB

Frequently served by doctors and dentists who don't know what else to do with the sweet sherry their patients give them. It's gorgeous.

1¼ cups heavy cream   grated rind and juice of 1 lemon
¼ cup sweet sherry   sugar to taste

Whip all the ingredients together and chill before serving.
Serves 3 to 4.

RUM AND LEMON SORBET

This sorbet is refreshing and good for summer lunch in the garden. (It can tolerate standing around in the sun for a while, being so hard and inedible when it comes out of the freezer.) If it is to be eaten on other occasions, take out of the freezer and store in the fridge for an hour or so before needed.

½ cup sugar   juice of 1 orange
1¼ cups water   1 tablespoon any kind of rum
rind and juice of 1 large lemon   1 egg white, stiffly beaten

Heat the sugar and water gently until the sugar dissolves. Continue cooking for another 10 minutes. Finely chop the rind and stir it into the syrup. Leave to cool.

When cold stir in the fruit juices and strain into a clean bowl. Keep in the freezer until almost frozen.

Then decant into another bowl, stir in the rum, and fold in a stiffly beaten egg white. Freeze until solid.
Serves 4.

MANDARIN GÂTEAU

Make a day or so in advance for best effect—it's rich, so please serve after a fairly light course.

¾ cup butter	about 20 ladyfingers (less than
1 cup sugar	2 packages) depending on size
1 tablespoon butter	of mold
1 tablespoon flour	8 tablespoons port
⅔ cup milk	1¼ cups heavy cream
2 small cans mandarin oranges	toasted almonds, chopped
1 egg	

Cream the ¾ cup of butter and sugar together until they are very pale and frothy. This can be tedious even with an electric beater, but some help can be gained by using butter which has been out of the fridge for an hour or two.

Make a white sauce with the other butter, flour, and milk. Over a low heat stir in the strained juice from one of the cans of mandarin oranges. Off the heat beat in the egg. Cover with a piece of greaseproof paper (to prevent a skin forming) and cool.

Mash the mandarin oranges from that can with a fork, and slowly beat them into the butter and sugar mixture with the sauce.

Dip each ladyfinger in the port and then line the base of a plastic box 10 inches by 5 inches (or 12 inches by 2 inches, or 8 inches by 4 inches, or similar). Spread half the filling over this layer. Dip the remaining fingers in the remaining port and layer again. Cover with the drained fruit from the second can. Spread the rest of the filling over this and chill.

Before serving whip the cream until fairly thick. Put the serving dish over the mold, turn it upside down, and shake the dessert out. Cover with cream and sprinkle with chopped toasted almonds.

Serves 8 plus.

MELON AND PINEAPPLE

Refreshing.

1 large honeydew melon
1 large can diced pineapple
¼ cup kirsch

Slice the top off the melon and keep it. Remove the seeds. Scoop out the flesh and dice it or use a special scoop to make melon balls. Put them in a bowl. Drain the pineapple and mix it with the melon and kirsch. Cut a slice off the bottom of the melon so that it will stand upright. Fill the melon shell with the mixture and replace the lid. Wrap well in aluminum foil before chilling in the fridge.
Serves up to 6.

MINTY MELON

This a little more exciting than serving a quarter of a melon per head; it is marginally more effort but well worth it.

1 small ripe melon   **⅔ cup sweet white wine**
2 tablespoons Rose's Lime Juice   few sprigs mint, chopped

Cut the top off the melon, spoon out the seeds, and then remove the flesh. Either do so with a little balling device or else remove in large chunks and dice the flesh. When you have taken out as much of the flesh as possible, gently mix it in a bowl with the lime juice, wine, and mint. Return to the shell, wrap in foil, and leave in the fridge until required.

This will happily keep for a day or two.
Serves 4.

GINGER MELON

Tasty, easy, and can be prepared well in advance. Do cover the melon in the fridge or smell problems occur.

1 cantaloupe	4 tablespoons brandy or rum
1½ teaspoons powdered ginger	1¼ cups heavy cream, whipped
½ cup sugar	

Cut the melon in half, scoop out the flesh, and dice or cut into balls. Keep the melon shells. Place the melon dice or balls in a bowl with the ginger and sugar. Cover and chill.

Before serving, add the brandy and pile into the melon shells. Serve with whipped cream.

Serves 4 to 6, depending on the size of the melon.

ORANGE AND GRAPEFRUIT CARAMEL

Very good.

2 grapefruit	2 tablespoons kirsch or Bols gin
2 oranges	soft brown sugar

Peel the fruit and remove all the pith. Skin the segments. Pack them evenly in a flameproof bowl and sprinkle with the liquor and enough brown sugar to cover to a depth of about ¼ inch.

Place under a hot grill for a couple of minutes until the sugar caramelizes, and either serve hot immediately, or chill it and serve cold.

Serves 4 to 6.

ORANGE FOOL

And a fool can make this perfect dessert.

4 oranges	**1 tablespoon any orange liqueur**
2 lemons	**or brandy**
2½ cups heavy cream	**8 dessert sponges**

Grate the rind of 2 oranges and 1 lemon. Liquidize all the fruit and strain it.

Beat the cream slightly and add the grated rinds. Add the fruit juice and liqueur. Line the dish in which the dessert is to be served with halved sponges (or ladyfingers) and pour the cream over them. Put in the fridge for at least 24 hours.

Serves 6.

ORANGE SALAD

This is excellent, easy, and everybody loves it.

8 oranges	**Cointreau, Grand Marnier, or**
2 cups sugar, maximum	**orange curaçao to taste**
1¼ cups water	

Peel the oranges with a very sharp knife to remove all the pith. (The easiest way is to cut off both ends, lay the orange flat on a board, and slice the peel off downwards in about 1-inch strips. This usually removes all the pith and skin together.)

Remove the pith from half the rind, and slice the rind into very thin strips. Melt the sugar in the water, stir, and bring to the boil. Boil until in a few minutes you have a thickish pale golden syrup. Add the strips of orange peel and continue cooking until almost caramelized. Cool, and add the liqueur. Pour over the oranges and serve chilled—with cream if wished. This should be done a day in advance.

Serves 4.

ORANGE JELLY

This is very light and cool—a perfect end to a heavy meal.

6 to 10 oranges (depending on size and juiciness)
orange liqueur to taste
1 envelope unflavored gelatin

Skin the oranges and put in a liquidizer. Add about ½ cup of water. Blend. Sieve into the bowl in which the dessert will be served. Add the liqueur.

Dissolve the gelatin in a little water. Stir it well into the juice. There must be *no* lumps. Leave to set in a cool place.

This will keep for some days and can be served with liqueur-enriched cream or on its own.

Serves 6.

HOT ORANGE SOUFFLÉ IN ORANGE SKINS

This is spectacular to look at, easy to cook, and good to eat.

6 large oranges plus the grated   **4 eggs, separated**
rind of 1 orange   **1 tablespoon sugar**
2 tablespoons butter   **2 tablespoons Cointreau or any**
3 teaspoons flour   **orange liqueur**
⅔ cup milk

Preheat the oven to 400° F. Cut the tops off the oranges at least a quarter way down. Using a rounded grapefruit knife, scoop out all the flesh and pour out the juice. Reserve. Stand the orange skins in tartlet tins to hold them upright.

Heat the butter, flour, and milk, stirring all the time. When thick, beat in the egg yolks, sugar, and grated orange rind. Then fold in the orange liqueur and stiffly beaten egg whites. Partly fill the orange skins, sprinkle a little sugar evenly over the top and bake for 5 minutes until golden on top.

Serves 6.

Use the orange flesh to make orange juice for breakfast or to make the recipe for Orange Jelly.

HOT CARAMEL ORANGES

This is delicious and no harder than grapefruit for breakfast.

4 large oranges (not thick-skinned and much nicer if seedless)
8 teaspoons Cointreau
a little sugar

Preheat oven to 350° F. Cut the oranges in half horizontally. Remove the core and loosen the segments with a grapefruit knife. Place, cut side upward, in a fireproof dish and pour 1 teaspoon of the liqueur into each. Cook in a medium oven for about ¼ hour. Remove.

Sprinkle a little sugar on the surface of each orange and place under a hot grill until the sugar caramelizes to a dark brown. Eat soon.

Serves 4.

You can omit the baking in the oven and just grill for longer—not quite so good—or you can substitute grapefruit for oranges, using sweet sherry instead of Cointreau.

POACHED PEACHES WITH RASPBERRY SAUCE

A delicious summer dessert.

8 ripe white peaches	**1½ pounds fresh raspberries**
2 cups water	**1 tablespoon kirsch**
½ cup granulated sugar	**blanched chopped almonds**
vanilla bean	

Parboil the peaches for about 1 minute, peel, and leave whole.

In a separate saucepan, boil the water, sugar, and vanilla for a few minutes. Remove the vanilla, and add the peaches and poach in the syrup over a low heat for 5 minutes. Remove to a serving dish.

Liquidize the raspberries and strain through a fine sieve. Sweeten the sauce with 2 to 3 tablespoons of the peach syrup and add the kirsch. Pour over the peaches and chill.

Before serving sprinkle with almonds.

Serves 4 to 8, depending on appetite.

PEACHES WITH MINCEMEAT AND WHISKY

This is an astonishingly good dessert which strains the culinary talent of no man.

1 large can peach halves	**8 tablespoons mincemeat**
(usually 8 halves)	**8 teaspoons whisky**
2 tablespoons whisky	

Preheat oven to 400° F. Drain the juice from the peaches into a pan. Pour about half of it away or drink it. Add 2 tablespoons of whisky.

Put the peaches, flat side up, in a large serving dish. Into the center of each put a spoonful of mincemeat and a teaspoon of whisky. Just before eating warm the syrup and whisky mixture, pour it over the fruit, and pop the lot into the oven for 5 minutes.

Serves 4 to 8, depending on your guests' greed.

PEACHES IN BRANDY

First invented on a wet camping holiday when both ingredients were very cheap.

at least 1 big peach per person
sugar
brandy—very inferior if that's all that's available

Ideally, peel the peaches. Slice. Put alternate layers of peach, sugar, and brandy in a container.

Leave for as long as you can bear. Serve with heavy cream if possible.

PEACH HEAVEN

This is always voted an absolute wow!

at least 1 big peach per person   **1 cup heavy cream, whipped**
   (canned will do)   **brown sugar**
brandy

Peel and slice the peaches into a fireproof dish. Add some brandy —not enough to soak the fruit. Coat with a thick layer of stiffly whipped cream. Leave in the fridge for several hours until the cream is pretty hard.

Sprinkle with a good layer of brown sugar.

Put under a very hot grill until the sugar caramelizes and trickles into the dissolving cream. Eat at once.

This recipe is equally good using grapes and whipping up the cream with brandy.

PEACHES IN RED WINE

Easy and expensive-looking but can be dirt cheap in the peach season.

6 to 9 yellow peaches
sugar
⅓ bottle dry red wine

Pour boiling water over the peaches and leave for a couple of minutes. Skin them and slice into individual goblets. Sprinkle with sugar and then pour the wine over them.
Serves 6.

SHERRY PEARS

You can't fail with this.

1¼ cups heavy cream
4 good eating pears
1 tablespoon sherry

1 heaped tablespoon sugar
sliced almonds or walnuts for
garnish

Pour the cream into a largish bowl and whip until thick but not stiff.

Peel and quarter the pears and very gently stir them into the cream, making sure they are well covered. Lift the pears from the cream and divide them among four glass dishes. Into the cream, beat the sugar and sherry. Pour it over the pears (using a rubber spatula to get it all up) and decorate with nuts. Chill.
Serves 4.

BLACK TREACLE PEARS

A marvelous recipe for using very hard pears (windfalls will do).

pears	cream
molasses	brandy
brown sugar	

Preheat oven to 250° F. or lower. Wash the pears and put them in a fireproof dish. (Do not peel or slice). Pour some molasses over them and sprinkle with brown sugar. Add a little water. Bake them covered, in a slow oven for about 3 to 4 hours. They should look wrinkled and brown—so don't fret.

Serve with the cream whipped with brandy.

Serves as many as you have pears for.

WINE-BAKED PEARS

Make this the night before your dinner party.

6 pears	sugar
⅓ bottle white wine	**1¼ cups heavy cream, whipped**

Preheat oven to 350° F. Peel the pears and put in a firepoof dish. Cover with the wine, sprinkle with a little sugar, and bake in the oven for about 45 minutes. Chill.

Serve with whipped cream.

Serves 6.

PORT-BAKED PLUMS

This recipe is nicer than stewed plums and requires the same effort.

1 pound slightly underripe plums	2 tablespoons water
3 tablespoons brown sugar	⅔ cup heavy cream
2 tablespoons port	

Preheat oven to 350° F. Wash the plums and split them along the dent. Put all the ingredients except the cream into an ovenproof dish and bake in the oven for about ¾ hour or until the plums are tender but still whole.

Serve hot or cold with cream.

Serves 3 to 4.

BRANDY PRUNE FOOL

There are many varieties of canned fruit in the shops: experiment with others, using this basic recipe.

2 medium-size cans prunes	2 tablespoons brandy
⅔ cup heavy cream	a few almonds to decorate

Stone the prunes and liquidize with half the juice. Whip the cream and add to the prunes, together with the brandy. Pour into individual glasses and decorate with almonds. Chill.

Serves 6.

RASPBERRY DELIGHT

If you are talented enough to make a cup of tea with a tea bag and boiling water, you'll be able to manage this no-trouble dessert.

1¼ cups heavy cream	1 pound raspberries (or 2
2 tablespoons sherry or kirsch	packages frozen)
1¼ cups plain yoghurt	

Whip the cream until stiff but not buttery. Add the liquor, fold in the yoghurt. Very gently stir in the raspberries—try not to break them all up—and pour into the bowl or bowls from which the dessert will be served. Chill in the fridge.

Serves 6.

Strawberries, loganberries, gooseberries, and others would be just as nice, though cook them or sweeten them as appropriate.

RASPBERRY GÂTEAU

You can just as easily use strawberries or any other fruit in season, varying the liqueur to suit what you use. This is simple to prepare and is much better for having been done well in advance.

½ cup butter	2 packages ladyfingers
½ cup sugar	kirsch
4 tablespoons almonds, ground	4 cups raspberries
4 tablespoons heavy cream	1 cup heavy cream, whipped

Line a 5- or 6-inch cake tin with a loose base with greaseproof paper.

Beat the butter and sugar until creamy, add the almonds, and beat a little longer. Stir in the 4 tablespoons of cream.

Cover the base of the tin with the ladyfingers. Sprinkle with the kirsch. Spread half the cream mixture on the fingers. Put the raspberries on top of the cream and sprinkle them with sugar (omit this if you've not a sweet tooth). Cover with the rest of the cream and press more ladyfingers gently on top. Sprinkle with kirsch.

Leave for at least 24 hours and then push gently out of the tin. Decorate with whipped cream and raspberries.

Serves 6.

RASPBERRY AND KIRSCH MOUSSE

This I love. Strawberries can be used instead of raspberries if there's a glut.

5 cups raspberries	1¼ cups heavy cream
a little sugar to taste	2 egg whites
2 tablespoons kirsch	pinch of salt

Put the raspberries into your liquidizer and purée them. Add a very little sugar and the kirsch. Keep covered.

Whisk the cream until thick and the egg whites until stiff (with the salt). Fold them together and leave in the fridge until they begin to set. Then whisk them again and fold in the purée.

Pour into a serving dish and leave in the fridge until required. *Serves 4 to 6.*

RHUBARB FOOL

More unusual than strawberry, etc., and can be made at a time of year when cold puddings are a comparative rarity.

2 pounds rhubarb	2½ cups heavy cream
6 tablespoons butter	1 tablespoon brandy or orange
1½ cups sugar	liqueur
1 tablespoon lemon juice	

Wash the rhubarb and cut it up. Melt the butter, add the sugar, rhubarb, and lemon juice and bring to the boil. Keep stirring until the fruit is soft but not slushy. Allow to cool.

Liquidize in a blender, then chill until just before you eat. Whip the cream, add the liqueur, and fold into the fruit mixture. If this is too sour (and deliberately it is not very sweet) add a little more sugar.

Serves 8.

STRAWBERRIES AND CREAM

This is a conventional idea prepared in an unconventional way.

7½ cups strawberries   1¼ cups heavy cream
granulated sugar   1¼ cups sour cream
2 tablespoons cherry brandy   pistachio nuts to decorate

Hull the strawberries and wash if necessary—I always avoid the latter if possible as they go so mushy. Put them in a bowl and sprinkle with the minimum of sugar. Add the liqueur and chill for several hours.

Just before serving, whisk the cream until it just begins to thicken and blend it with the sour cream (which should not be whisked). Pour the cream over the strawberries and sprinkle with chopped nuts.

Serves 6 to 8.

STRAWBERRY AND ORANGE DESSERT

The fruits complement each other beautifully.

3 oranges   2 tablespoons lemon juice
4 cups strawberries   2 tablespoons Grand Marnier or
1 cup sugar   Cointreau
⅔ cup water

Cut a slice off the top and bottom of the oranges and then place them on a flat board and cut downward with a knife to remove the peel and pith. Slice the oranges thinly, remove all pips, and place in a serving dish. Hull the strawberries and arrange over the oranges.

Melt the sugar in the water over a low heat, stirring constantly. Remove from heat and add the lemon juice and the liqueur. Allow to cool and then pour over the fruit and chill.

Serves 6.

STRAWBERRY CREAM

A nice dinner-party sweet to serve when strawberries alone are no longer a treat.

6 cups strawberries	1 tablespoon light rum
¼ cup sugar	1¼ cups heavy cream
1 tablespoon kirsch	1 quart vanilla ice cream,
1 tablespoon Cointreau	slightly soft

Wipe, or wash, and hull the strawberries. In a serving bowl crush them slightly and add the sugar and the three liquors.

Whip the cream and mix together with the ice cream. Pour this over the strawberries and leave to chill for about ½ hour.

Serves a good 8.

STRAWBERRY JELLY

This is nearly as nice as wild strawberries sprinkled with wine but sadly wild strawberries don't happen very often.

4 cups strawberries	½ bottle sweet white wine
juice of ½ lemon	1 envelope unflavored gelatin
a little sugar	

Halve the strawberries and arrange them in a suitable bowl. Sprinkle with the lemon juice and sugar.

Heat the wine, being careful not to boil it, and add the gelatin, which has already been dissolved in a very little hot water. Stir occasionally until the wine is cool. Pour over the strawberries and leave to set.

This is better served without cream.

Serves 4 to 6.

BAVARIAN STRAWBERRY FLAN

Easy and can be made a day in advance.

6 cups strawberries (strained canned ones can also be used)	**1 tablespoon Grand Marnier**
3 tablespoons sugar	**1¼ cups heavy cream**
1 envelope unflavored gelatin	**sugar**
4 tablespoons cold water	**pinch of salt**
	1 bought large sponge flan case

Hull the strawberries and, keeping aside a few for decoration, mash them. Stir in sugar to taste. Dissolve the gelatin in the water, stir into the strawberry mixture, and add the liqueur. Put this into the fridge until it begins to thicken slightly.

Meanwhile whisk the cream with a little sugar and a pinch of salt until thick but not buttery. Add the strawberry mixture and fill the flan with it. Chill.

Decorate with whole strawberries and fresh sprigs of mint if available.

Serves 6 to 8.

ELIZABETHAN FLAN

And it's delicious.

2 large thin-skinned oranges	**⅔ cup heavy cream**
2 tablespoons honey	**1 tablespoon brandy**
⅔ cup water	**¼ cup sugar**
½ pound rich pastry	

Wash the oranges and cut into thin rings with the peel left on. Soak overnight in honey and water. Next day place the oranges and liquid in a pan and simmer for about ½ hour. Drain and cool, keeping the liquid.

Preheat oven to 350° F. Put an 8-inch flan dish on a baking sheet and line with the pastry. Bake "blind," i.e. cover with grease-proof paper and fill with rice or beans to weigh it down, for 15 minutes. Remove the paper and filling and cook for a further 10 minutes until pale gold. Cool.

Whip the cream until just stiff, add the brandy, and spread over the bottom of the flan case. Overlap the orange slices on top. Add the sugar to ⅔ cup of the honey liquid and heat gently until the sugar has dissolved. Bring to the boil and cook until syrupy, probably a maximum of 5 minutes. Pour this gently over the oranges and cream.

Serves 4 to 6.

RUM AND CHOCOLATE FLAN

This benefits by being made in advance so that the ice cream can melt a little, which makes it easier to spread.

4 ounces semisweet chocolate	**4 tablespoons rum**
2 cups cornflakes	**1 pint chocolate ripple ice cream**
1½ cups cake crumbs	

Melt three quarters of the chocolate in a non-stick pan and gently stir in the cornflakes until they are evenly coated with chocolate. Spread a 6-inch soufflé dish with the mixture and chill.

Mix the crumbs with the rum and spread on top of the cornflakes. Spread the ice cream on top of this and decorate with the rest of the chocolate, grated. Chill until wanted.

Serves 6.

AULD ALLIANCE CREAM

This is delicious, very easy (except that you have to think about it two days in advance), and, provided there is a whisky drinker in the house, very cheap.

1¼ cups prunes	1¼ cups hot water
1¼ cups water	1 package lemon-flavored gelatin
½ cup whisky	1 1-inch cinnamon stick
grated rind and juice of ½ lemon	4 cloves
¼ teaspoon ground ginger	whipped cream and nuts to
1 good tablespoon sugar	decorate

Wash the prunes and soak them in the water and whisky for a couple of days. (Omit the water if they are the moist variety.) Don't cook them. Then remove the stones if necessary and liquidize until smooth. Stir in the lemon rind and juice, ginger, and sugar.

Pour the hot water over the gelatin, cinnamon, and cloves. Stir until dissolved; if necessary reheat a little. Allow to cool.

Strain the liquid into the prune mixture and leave until it starts to set. Stir well. Pour into individual glasses or one large bowl. Decorate with whipped cream and nuts.

Serves 6.

BISKOTTEN TORTE

*This is a rich pudding which takes some time to prepare but is very
easy. It is much better made a couple of days before you need it,
but do allow at least 24 hours or the full taste doesn't emerge.*

¾ cup butter	2 tablespoons flour
1 cup sugar	⅔ cup milk
1 egg	4 tablespoons brandy or Tia
½ cup walnuts and a few	Maria
more for decoration	2 packages ladyfingers
1½ teaspoons instant coffee	1 cup milk
powder	1¼ cups heavy cream for
2 tablespoons butter	decoration

Beat the butter and sugar vigorously. When pale add the egg and
continue beating until creamy. Mince the walnuts and add with
the coffee powder.

Melt the butter, add the flour, and cook gently for 1 minute.
Add the milk all at once and cook for 5 minutes, stirring continuously. Leave to cool. Then add a spoonful at a time to the walnut
mixture.

Line a 6-inch cake tin with greaseproof paper.

Add the liqueur to the milk. Dip the ladyfingers very lightly in
the mixture. (Be careful not to saturate the fingers or they become
soggy and unpalatable.) Line the bottom and sides of the tin with
them. Then fill the tin with a layer of walnut cream, dipped fingers,
walnut cream, and end with dipped fingers. Cover with greaseproof
paper and put in the fridge.

Turn out gently (it can collapse). Whip the cream and ice the
pudding with it. Decorate with walnuts if desired (ground if you
have the time).

Serves 8 to 10.

CALVADOS GLORY

*This concoction was invented on the spur of the moment when a
load of uninvited guests turned up to be fed. It was immediately
successful and required very little effort. Try it.*

1 package ladyfingers	**⅔ cup heavy cream**
1 tablespoon Calvados	**almonds to garnish (optional)**
½ pound apple jelly	

Line a shallow serving dish with the ladyfingers. Sprinkle with
Calvados. Warm the jelly to the point where it is no longer solid.
There is no need to melt it entirely. Spread this over the fingers as
evenly as possible. Put the mixture in the fridge to cool off. Whip
the cream; you can thin it down with a little light cream as well.
Spread this over your dessert, decorate with nuts if you care to,
and serve when you will.
Serves 4 to 6.

CHEESE FREEZE

Child's play and rich.

⅔ cup heavy cream	**8 ounces black cherry jam**
⅔ cup cottage cheese	**1 to 2 tablespoons kirsch**

Whip the cream until stiff and stir into the cheese. Spoon it into individual ramekins and freeze. Just before serving heat the jam
with the kirsch. Either pour the sauce into each ramekin or pass it
separately.
Serves 4 to 6, depending on the size of the ramekins.
This can also be made with marmalade and whisky.

RICH GLORIOUS CHOCOLATE MOUSSE

Never fails, always pleases.

6 ounces semisweet chocolate	2 tablespoons brandy
1 tablespoon water	salt
5 eggs	

In a double pan melt the broken-up chocolate with the water. Cook gently, stirring vigorously until the chocolate is smooth. Allow to cool to body temperature. Separate the eggs and beat in the yolks one by one. Stir in the liqueur.

Whisk the egg whites with a pinch of salt. When stiff, fold them into the mousse. Either pour into a glass serving dish or distribute among individual dishes.

This serves 6, but if you arrange a layer of brandy-soaked ladyfingers at the bottom of your serving dish or dishes, it will easily feed 8.

CHOCOLATE BRANDY TRIFLE (1)

A good rich pudding that should be served very cold.

6 ounces semisweet chocolate	3 tablespoons brandy
1 cup milk	a handful of macaroons, chopped
1 package ladyfingers	1¼ cups heavy cream

Grate two thirds of the chocolate. Melt the remaining chocolate in the milk over a low heat. Cool.

Line a large shallow dish with the ladyfingers. Mix the brandy into the chocolate and pour the lot over the fingers. Sprinkle with the macaroons.

Whip the cream and fold in most of the grated chocolate. Pile this into the bowl and decorate with the remaining chocolate.

Serves 6 to 8.

CHOCOLATE BRANDY TRIFLE (2)

A variation on the previous recipe.

2 packages ladyfingers	6 ounces semisweet chocolate
3 tablespoons sherry	a little water
3 tablespoons brandy	1¼ cups heavy cream

Dip the fingers in the sherry and brandy and arrange in a row across a serving bowl.

Melt most of the chocolate in water and pour some of it over the fingers. Arrange another row of dipped fingers at right angles to the first. Cover with chocolate. Continue until supplies run out. (The number of layers depends on the size and shape of the bowl.)

Whip the cream and pile on top of the layers. Grate the remaining chocolate and sprinkle over the cream.

Serves 6 to 8.

CHOCOLATE SLUDGE

A descriptive but inelegant title which shouldn't put you off this rich dessert. But don't serve it after two heavy courses—your guests won't be happy.

6 tablespoons kirsch
1 cup petit beurre biscuits, crumbled
8 ounces chocolate chips or semisweet chocolate
4 tablespoons water
¾ cup butter

4 eggs, separated
1 cup confectioners' sugar
1 cup grapes, peeled (or drained canned grapes)
1¼ cups cream
confectioners' sugar to decorate

Sprinkle the kirsch over the biscuit crumbs and leave to soak.

Very gently dissolve the chocolate in the water. Stir until smooth and then take off the heat. Gradually add the butter, stir until the chocolate absorbs it all. Add the egg yolks and stir until smooth, then repeat with the 1 cup sugar. Beat the egg whites until stiff and then add them. Stir in the crumb mixture and the grapes. Finally add the cream.

Oil a loose-bottomed cake tin and line it with oiled greaseproof paper. Pour in the mixture and chill.

Immediately before serving, turn out and dredge with confectioners' sugar.

This is, par excellence, a dessert that can be made well in advance.

Serves 8.

COFFEE MARSHMALLOW WITH BRANDY CREAM

A rather interesting dessert that amuses people who never guess what makes it jell.

40 marshmallows
1¼ cups very strong instant black coffee
1¼ cups heavy cream

1 tablespoon brandy
chopped almonds or walnuts for decoration

Cut the marshmallows up into four (marginally sticky job, easiest when done with kitchen scissors dipped in water). Put them in a large bowl with the boiling coffee. Whisk until they dissolve and the mixture froths. Turn into a large serving bowl or individual glasses. Allow to cool.

Whip the cream until fairly stiff. Add the brandy. Spread over the dessert and decorate with almonds or walnuts, as you will.

Serves 6 to 8.

GIN TORTE

Gin is not widely used in cooking, but having tasted this you'll long to find more excuses for flavoring with gin.

¾ cup sugar
3 eggs
½ cup butter
4 tablespoons almonds, ground
½ cup cake flour

icing:
½ cup confectioners' sugar
1 generous tablespoon gin

Preheat oven to 425° F. Beat the sugar and eggs until thick and fluffy. Soften the butter. Work it into the mixture together with the almonds and flour. Mix thoroughly.

Bake in a well-buttered tin for 15 minutes until firm. Cool.

Just before serving mix the confectioners' sugar with the gin and spread on top of the cake. If you do this too far in advance you will sadly lose the aroma of the liquor.

Serves 4 to 6.

PORT JELLY

So many people have never tasted anything but commercial jellies, they'll be delighted by the soft flavor and texture of this one.

½ cup sugar
1¼ cups water
1 tablespoon red currant or
   apple jelly
1 inch or so cinnamon stick

3 cloves
juice and thinly pared rind of
   1 lemon
1 envelope unflavored gelatin
1¼ cups port

In a scrupulously clean pan gently heat the sugar, water, jelly, cinnamon, cloves, and juice and rind of the lemon.

Dissolve the gelatin in a very little water and stir that in. Then continue simmering a few minutes longer. Stir in the port.

Strain through muslin until clear (a sieve will do, though the results won't look quite so good). Allow to cool a little.

Then rinse the jelly mold in cold water and pour the jelly in. Leave to set. Turn out just before serving.

Serves 4.

GINGER WINE JELLY

Ginger wine is traditionally drunk with Scotch whisky to make a whisky mac, but it is surprisingly good made into this light dessert. Ginger wine can be got from the better liquor stores—distribution is increasing all the time.

1 cup cold water	**3 tablespoons sugar**
1 envelope unflavored gelatin	**1¼ cups Stone's Ginger Wine**
juice and thinly pared rind of	**whipped cream**
1 lemon	**ladyfingers**

Put the water into a saucepan, add the gelatin, and leave for a few minutes. Add the lemon rind and heat slowly, stirring all the time, until all the gelatin has dissolved. Add the sugar and dissolve.

Remove from heat and leave to stand for about 10 minutes. Add the ginger wine and lemon juice and leave to cool. Strain through muslin into individual glasses. Chill. Decorate with a layer of cream and serve with ladyfingers.

Serves 4.

LIQUEUR SOUFFLÉ

Very simple, and it can all be prepared in advance except for beating the egg whites.

spongecake	3½ tablespoons sugar
liqueur	1 tablespoon liqueur
4 eggs	

Preheat oven to 400° F. Line a soufflé dish with a thin layer of spongecake, and sprinkle it liberally with liqueur. Separate the eggs. Beat the yolks until they pale. Add the sugar and keep beating; when they are creamy add the 1 tablespoon of liqueur.

Beat the egg whites until stiff. Fold the two mixtures together and pour into a soufflé dish. Bake for 10 minutes.

(If you use orange liqueur, add the grated rind of 1 orange.)
Serves 4.

FROSTED LIQUEUR MOUSSE

Good summer dessert.

1 large egg white	a few chopped nuts, toasted
1¼ cups heavy cream	
2 level tablespoons confectioners' sugar, sifted	
2 tablespoons apricot brandy, Chartreuse, Grand Marnier, rum, or really any strongly flavored liqueur	

Whisk the egg white until stiff. In another bowl whisk the cream until it is just beginning to thicken, add the sugar, and continue whipping until the cream is thick but not too stiff. Fold in the egg white and the liqueur. Spoon into individual dishes, sprinkle with nuts, and freeze until firm.

Serves 4.

NORWEGIAN CREAM

This is especially good served after something like a very hot curry, as it is light and rather bland.

2 cups milk	3 tablespoons apricot jam
1½ tablespoons sugar	2 tablespoons apricot brandy
3 eggs	3 tablespoons cream
2 or 3 drops vanilla extract	grated chocolate

Preheat oven to 350° F. Boil the milk with the sugar. Keep back 1 egg white and put the other eggs and whites in a separate bowl. Beat slightly with vanilla extract. Pour over the milk when hot but not boiling.

Put the jam and brandy in the bottom of an ovenproof dish. Pour in the strained custard. Stand in water and bake, covered, until set. Remove from the oven.

When cold beat the remaining egg white, fold it into the cream. Beat the cream and cover the pudding. Sprinkle with grated chocolate.

Serves 4.

GINGER BRANDY

This dessert is even more glorious if allowed to chill for about 48 hours.

  2 cups heavy cream
  2 packages gingersnaps
  1 cup strong black coffee doused with brandy

Whip the cream until stiff. Dip the snaps in the coffee mixture one by one and put alternate layers of snaps and cream until all ingredients are used, making sure to leave enough cream aside to decorate the top just before serving (so that it doesn't go brown).

Cover the pudding, preferably with a weighted plate, and leave to chill overnight or preferably much longer.

Decorate with cream before serving.

Serves 8.

PUFF PASTRY GÂTEAU

This looks most professional and is so easy and quick to make.

  1 package frozen puff pastry
  ⅔ cup heavy cream
  1 tablespoon fruit liqueur or sherry

  fresh or canned fruit
  confectioners' sugar, sieved, for decoration

Preheat oven to 350° F. Roll the pastry until extremely thin—should be a rectangular shape. Bake for about 20 minutes, or until it has risen and is golden on the outside and cooked inside. Remove from the oven and slit with a knife lengthways in half. If this should reveal some uncooked pastry on the inside, either remove it or put the two halves back into the oven at a low heat to dry out.

Whip the cream together with the liqueur and add the fruit. When the pastry has cooled, fill the case with the fruit mixture, put the lid on top, and sprinkle with sieved confectioners' sugar.

Serves 4.

CRÊPES SUZETTE

A world-favorite spectacular, easily made in this way.

1½ cups flour	¾ cup sugar
3 eggs	finely grated rind of 1 or 2
1½ tablespoons sugar	oranges
2 cups milk	3 tablespoons orange liqueur
1½ tablespoons good oil	plus 4 or 5 more tablespoons
1½ tablespoons brandy	brandy or liqueur to flame
10 tablespoons butter	

Preheat oven to 400° F. Sift the flour into a large bowl and break the eggs into the middle of it. Stir them until the mixture is smooth, then add the 1½ tablespoons of sugar and the milk. You are supposed to leave the mixture to stand for a couple of hours but I never do, and it doesn't seem to matter. Just before cooking stir in the oil and brandy and mix well. Melt a little butter in a small pan and fry as many very thin pancakes as you can get out of the mixture.

Meanwhile, with a fork, mash the remaining butter and ¾ cup of sugar, and when well mixed add the orange rind and liqueur.

As each pancake is made, spread it with a little of the butter mixture. Roll the pancakes up and arrange in an ovenproof dish. When all are made, sprinkle with a little sugar and try to keep fairly warm. Put in a hot oven for less than 10 minutes, and at the table pour hot brandy or liqueur over them, ignite, and consume at once. Quite delicious.

Serves 6.

PANCAKES FILLED WITH FRUIT

This is delicious, filling, and impressive-looking. Making the pancakes is far more boring than making the filling.

8 small thin pancakes	2 tablespoons apricot jam
2 tablespoons butter	⅓ cup heavy cream
very little lemon juice	2 tablespoons Calvados
2 apples	few macaroons

Having made the pancakes, stack them on a Pyrex dish one on top of another, separated by greaseproof paper. Put the dish on a pan of hot water and keep it hot. A piece of foil loosely over the lot ensures that they stay warm without getting soggy.

Melt the butter with the lemon juice. Peel, core, and chop the apples, add to the butter, and cook them until soft. Then stir in the jam. Whip the cream, stir in the Calvados, and add to the apple mixture. This is the stuffing.

Fill the pancakes, roll them up, and arrange in a fireproof dish. Sprinkle with crushed macaroons and a little sugar and leave under a hot grill until caramelly on top (this takes no time at all). Eat at once.

Serves 4.

RUM OMELET

When I was a little girl living in Malta we used to lunch out at least two Sundays a month at the Melitta Hotel. I always had rum omelets, which were probably the first alcoholic desserts I came across. This is how they were made—I remember finding out at the time.

4 eggs	sugar for garnish
1 tablespoon sugar	3 tablespoons rum
pinch of salt	
2 tablespoons dark jam: cherry, strawberry, or plum	

Separate the eggs. Stir the yolks with the sugar, beat the whites with the salt until stiff, and fold into the yolk mixture. Cook the omelet, fill with the warmed jam, fold over, slide onto a fireproof dish, and sprinkle with sugar. Then place it under a hot grill for a second or two. Meanwhile warm the rum, pour it over the omelet, set it alight, and eat at once. Heaven.

Serves 2.

Some schools of thought omit the jam, others don't separate the eggs or beat the egg whites. Still others fill their omelet with warmed fruit rather than jam. Many people like more sugar, still others prefer their omelets flamed with Pernod or scented spirits. All are good, but I have my loyalties.

HOT GINGER SOUFFLÉ

Comparatively unusual.

3 tablespoons butter	⅛ pound preserved ginger,
3 tablespoons flour	chopped
1¼ cups milk	4 eggs
½ cup sugar	whipped cream
1 tablespoon brandy	preserved ginger in syrup
a good pinch powdered ginger	

Preheat oven to 350° F. Make a thick white sauce with the butter, flour, and milk and cook for a couple of minutes. Add the sugar, brandy, and both gingers. Separate the eggs, and beat yolks into the mixture one at a time. Whisk the egg whites until stiff and then fold them into the mixture. Pour into a prepared 7-inch soufflé dish.

Bake for about 45 minutes or until well risen and firm on top. Serve at once with whipped cream and/or ginger in syrup.

Serves a good 4.

CHOCOLATE RUM SOUFFLÉ

Very rich, very delicious.

2½ cups milk	1 envelope unflavored gelatin
6 medium eggs	4 tablespoons water
½ cup cake flour	1¼ cups heavy cream
1 cup sugar	4 ounces semisweet chocolate
4½ ounces semisweet chocolate	for decoration (optional)
2 tablespoons rum	

Heat the milk until almost boiling (do not boil). Separate the eggs and set aside the whites. In the top of a double saucepan beat together the egg yolks, flour, and sugar. Then add the milk and stir until the mixture thickens. Grate the 4½ ounces of chocolate and add to the mixture. Remove from the heat and stir until the chocolate has melted. Beat vigorously and add the rum. Pour into a large bowl.

Completely dissolve the gelatin in the boiling water and beat into the mixture. Whip the cream, and add to the mixture. Whisk the egg whites until stiff and fold in.

Place the bowl in a larger bowl of ice and whip the whole mixture until it begins to wrinkle.

Scotch tape a piece of foil around a soufflé dish with 3 inches jutting over the top, pour the soufflé into the dish and leave to set in a cool place.

If you have time, decorate with chocolate leaves made by washing a few rose leaves, melting 4 ounces of semisweet chocolate in a non-stick pan, and coating one side of the leaves by dragging them over the chocolate. Allow them to cool and then peel off the leaves.

Serves 6 to 8.

SHERRY CREAM

Should anyone give you some sweet sherry and should you not be too keen on sweet sherry, you can use it to make up this recipe of Helen Burke's which is both very good and very easy—much nicer than drinking sweet sherry.

1 envelope unflavored gelatin	¼ cup sugar
6 tablespoons water	salt
8 tablespoons sweet sherry	1¼ cups heavy cream
4 eggs	

Soak the gelatin in the water, then dissolve it over a low heat. Add the sherry.

Separate the eggs. Beat the yolks and sugar until they are fluffy, and then stir in the gelatin mixture. Add a tiny pinch of salt to the whites and beat them till stiff. Fold them into the mixture. Then beat the cream (don't bother washing the whisk) until it is thick but not stiff. Fold that in too. Turn into the serving dish and chill.

Serves 8.

If this is made a day or so ahead of time take it out of the fridge well in advance of the meal or it will be too stiff.

WHISKY CREAM

Where this recipe originated I don't know, but since a magazine published it about a year ago I seem to have eaten it at most people's homes.

1 envelope unflavored gelatin	2 good tablespoons honey
⅔ cup cold water	4 tablespoons whisky
2½ cups heavy cream	

Dissolve the gelatin in the water. Whip the cream until fairly thick. Gently whip the honey and the whisky. Fold in the dissolved gelatin, keep folding until the mixture starts to set. You have to persevere or it will separate a bit. Pour into individual serving dishes (it looks pretty in glass) and chill.
Serves 8.

WHISKY AND OATMEAL SYLLABUB

Attractive.

⅔ cup uncooked oatmeal	5 tablespoons whisky
1¼ cups heavy cream	1 teaspoon lemon juice
4 tablespoons honey	

Sprinkle the oatmeal onto a flat fireproof dish and toast under the grill until golden, shaking occasionally so that it does not burn.

Whip the cream until stiff. Mix together the honey, whisky, and lemon juice, add to the cream, and whip until very stiff. Fold in half the oatmeal. Pile the mixture into glasses and chill. Sprinkle with the remaining oatmeal before serving.
Serves 6.

HOT ZABAGLIONE

Making this is a knack. If you've got it you serve a memorable pudding; if not, the dog has boozy scrambled eggs for supper.

6 egg yolks   **5 tablespoons Marsala**
¼ cup sugar   **ladyfingers**

Put the first three ingredients in a double saucepan, making quite sure that the top half doesn't touch the water. Whisk over a low heat until the mixture lightens in color and thickens in texture. Pour immediately into individual glasses and serve with the lady-fingers. It must be eaten immediately.
Serves 6.

STILTON WITH PORT

Should you have bought a whole Stilton cheese and be left with all the crumbling bits, this is so good you might also be tempted to go out and buy Stilton to make it from scratch.
It is currently very smart to sneer at it, but try it for yourself—I like it.

Stilton cheese
port

Mash however much Stilton you have with a fork. Then add the port little by little and mash it in. Get the cheese to take as much wine as possible. Pack it into a serving dish and eat with biscuits.

CREAM CHEESE WITH WINE

This is a more mundane alternative to the Stilton with port but is still good.

1 pound cream cheese	½ cup not too dry white wine
¼ cup sugar	juice of 1 lemon

Mash the cheese, then gradually work in the sugar, wine, and lemon juice. This is also served with biscuits.
Serves 4 plus.

BLACK FOREST ICE CREAM

This German recipe is simple and good.

1 can black cherries	⅔ cup heavy cream
1 tablespoon kirsch	a few almonds for decoration
1 pint vanilla ice cream	

Strain the juice from the cherries into a pan with the kirsch. Warm it.

Meanwhile divide the ice cream into four and put each portion into the bottom of a sundae glass. Divide the cherries among the glasses.

Whip the cream until thick. Spoon that over the ice cream and cherries, by which time the juice ought to be just the right temperature (not so hot as to melt everything at once). Pour that over the top, sprinkle with almonds, and serve at once.
Serves 4.

PEPPERMINT CHOCOLATE ICE

This is equally good made with either cream or ice cream and couldn't be easier.

  1 quart vanilla ice cream or 2½ cups whipped cream
  2 ounces semisweet chocolate, grated
  3 to 4 tablespoons crème de menthe

Allow the ice cream to thaw slightly. Mix all the ingredients together and decorate with a little additional grated chocolate. Freeze.
  Serves 6.

RUM AND RAISIN ICE CREAM

This has to be prepared at least 3 hours in advance, but apart from that slight complication, it takes longer to wash up than make.

  1 quart vanilla ice cream
  2 tablespoons rum
  ⅔ cup raisins

Allow the ice cream to thaw slightly. Stir in the other ingredients. Pour into a serving dish. Freeze.
  (If you have time, the raisins are delicious soaked in the rum beforehand.)
  Serves 6.

ZABAGLIONE ICE CREAM

These two Helen Burke recipes make delicious ice cream, but as they are made from frozen cream, they must be taken out of the freezer at least 15 minutes before serving—or they won't taste quite so good.

3 large egg yolks	⅔ cup heavy cream
3 heaping teaspoons sugar	chopped toasted almonds to
4 tablespoons Marsala	decorate

Beat the egg yolks and sugar until creamy. Add the Marsala and beat over a pan of hot water (but do not let the bowl touch the water or the mixture will scramble) until fairly stiff. Take off the heat and continue beating until cold. Whip the cream and fold into the mixture. Pour into a suitable vessel and freeze.
Serves 4.

A KIND OF CASSATA

Excellent.

2 tablespoons currants	1 tablespoon chopped almonds
2 tablespoons raisins	1 tablespoon brandy
1 tablespoon orange peel, chopped	1 tablespoon orange juice
1 tablespoon glacé cherries, chopped	1¼ cups heavy cream
	1 tablespoon confectioners' sugar

Soak the fruit and nuts in the brandy and orange juice in a screw-top jar overnight. Shake it every now and then.

Whip the cream and sugar until fairly stiff. Fold in the fruit and mix well. Pour it into a pretty dish and freeze.
Serves 4 or 5.

INDEX

Alcohol (alcoholic beverages), use in cooking of, xi–xiii
See also specific kinds, recipes
Ale stew, brown, 53
Anchovies and port, beef with, 55
Appetizer(s)
  shrimp and mushroom, 37
  See also Starters (first courses)
Appetizing pears, 13
Apple(s)
  baked with rum and apricot jam, 114
  and blackberry mousse, extra special, 119
  curry soup, 22
  desert, delicious, 114
  duck with, 93
  oats, toffee, 115
  pheasant with cream and, 96
  stewed in cider, 115
Apricot(s)
  ice cream pudding, 117
  omelet, French, 113
  and orange fool, 117
  soufflé, hot, 116
  sweet and sour, 116
Artichoke(s)
  chilled veal with, 85
  mousse, Jerusalem, 4
Asparagus sauce, ham in, 66
Auld Alliance cream, 147
Avocado(s)
  and egg and sherry mousse, 8
  with grapes, 3
  iced soup, 22–23
  mousse, 3

Baked
  apples with rum and apricot jam, 114
  chops with nuts and vegetables, 77
  eggs
    in mushroom sauce, 7

    with mustard, cheese, and wine, 6
    with pâté, 6
  fillet of sole, 105
  pears, wine-, 139
  plums, wine-, 140
Banana(s)
  cream, 118
  flambéed, 118–19
Bavarian strawberry flan, 145
Beef
  with anchovies and port, 55
  hot pot, mother-in-law's, 52–53
  roast, gravy for, xi–xii, 47
  stew(s)
    brown ale, 53
    "leftover," 51
  Stroganoff, 41
  See also Boeuf; Ground beef; Meat; Steak; specific recipes
Biskotten torte, 148
Blackberry and apple mousse, extra special, 119
Black cherry tipsy trifle, 120–21
Black Forest ice cream, 166
Black treacle pears, 139
Bloody Mary soup, 23
Boeuf
  en croûte, 54
  en daube, 50–51
  au Grand Marnier, 52
  à la Marseilles, 50
  See also Beef
Bolognese, spaghetti, 46
Boned chicken in wine, 60–61
Boozy pheasant, 95
Bordelaise sauce, grilled steak with, 49
Braised
  ham with Madeira, 64
  salmon in white wine, 106
Brandied shrimps with rice, 34

P